Praise for *Create A*

"Alan Seale brilliantly brings together ancient wisdom with quantum understanding for practical application in daily life and leadership. Step by step, he unfolds the anatomy of transformation and shows us how to develop a personal presence that is transformational in service of a greater good."
— PATRICIA ABURDENE, author of *Megatrends* 2010

"Alan Seale's new book overflows with wisdom and gives you a roadmap so you can have heaven, here, now, on our earth. Enrich yourself and the world by reading it and then telling those who share your dream."
— MARTIN RUTTE, co-author of *Chicken Soup for the Soul at Work*, founder of Project Heaven on Earth

"Seale weaves together the cocreative principles governing human culture in ways that will alter how you embody and express the evolutionary intelligence within yourself and the Universe. Few are the guides to this terrain who possess the intuition, compassion, and brilliance for activating the developmental potential of the human spirit."
— MICHAEL BERNARD BECKWITH, author of *Spiritual Liberation: Fulfilling Your Soul's Potential* and spiritual director of Agape

"Compelling, inspirational, and concisely presented! Alan Seale has done a fabulous job of providing a powerful roadmap for those who are serious about living the transformative life."
— JOHN RENESCH, global futurist, author of *Getting to the Better Future: A Matter of Conscious Choosing*

"*Create A World That Works* shows how you and I, every one of us can transform to be the architects of the world we can now create. Read it, and be the change we all need in the world."
— ERVIN LASZLO, author of *Chaos Point 2012 and Beyond*

"There's a new world fast approaching that will require new humans – individuals who have mastered the practicalities of operating in a full-spectrum, physical-spiritual environment. This guidebook is a manual for becoming someone new."
— JOHN L. PETERSEN, publisher and editor of *FUTUREdition*, founder and president of The Arlington Institute

"Alan Seale's ability to combine ancient wisdom with modern knowledge and experience makes him a master at building bridges of understanding and action."

—Anna Lena Smith, Director of Training,
CoachWalk Academy, Malmö, Sweden

"Alan Seale shows us that creating an authentic relationship with ourselves gives us a powerful relationship with the world . . . an approach to transformation that scales from personal to global."

—Mel Toomey, LHD, founder, Center for Leadership Studies,
scholar in residence at the Graduate Institute

"Alan Seale proposes a model for transformational leadership that works by cocreating the change that wants to happen. Instead of planning to meet today's changes with yesterday's information, leaders will find themselves working backward from tomorrow's potential to what needs to happen today in order to get there."

—Rev. Peter Heinrichs, United Church of Christ minister

"*Create A World That Works* is all about moving from the deeply personal awareness and presence to the powerful impact I create around me. If Alan Seale can live it, so can I. And so can everyone else. This is the way we create a world that works."

—Tine Gaihede, director, European Leadership, Copenhagen

"Underlying all of what Alan Seale is saying is the deep belief of our interconnectedness. This is a must-read book for anyone called to make a difference in today's world."

—Marita Fridjhon, ORSCC, MSW, PCC, CPCC,
co-founder and CEO of CRR Global

"Doors to a fuller life will open to you that you never imagined existed, and your life will become the blessing to the world it was designed to be."

—Rev. Sally Hamlin, minister,
First Universalist Church of Rochester, New York

". . . A masterful blending of scientific knowledge, spiritual wisdom, and practical tools. Its genius is in laying out a universal guide that can be applied across a variety of settings."

—Philip M. Hellmich, senior officer, Strategic Philanthropy
Search for Common Ground

"... Probably the single most important book I have read on prophetic leadership. Be prepared to discover and claim your own unique transformational power as you embark upon the journey of these pages."

—Rev. Amy Gopp, executive director of Week of Compassion

"If you want to be a part of creating a world that works, read this book."

—Cynthia Loy Darst, CPCC, ORSCC, MCC, coach and trainer

"... If you take on even a small portion of what is offered here, it will make a profound difference."

—Judi Neal, PhD, director, Tyson Center for Faith and Spirituality in the Workplace, Sam M. Walton College of Business, University of Arkansas

"Imagine what could happen if business and government leaders took these tools and perspectives to heart. Now that would create a world that works!"

—Alice Larsen, president, New Day Company, Zürich, Switzerland

"Alan Seale has managed to take grace and genius and distill it into concrete and immediately applicable steps."

—Tama J. Kieves, bestselling author of *This Time I Dance! Creating the Work You Love (How One Harvard Lawyer Left It All to Have It All!)*

"*Create A World That Works* is profound, actionable, and concrete."

—Jakob Algreen-Ussing, founder of Akasha Ventures, author of *The Quantum Company*

"In challenging times such as these, the world needs more books like *Create A World That Works!*"

—Daniel Karslake, director and producer of *Every Three Seconds* and *For the Bible Tells Me So*

"This is a vast tool kit filled with clearly articulated models, exercises, processes, and step-by-step instructions for how to unleash your energy and focus it into what you are most passionate about, thereby helping to create a world that works."

—Peter J. Reding, author of *Positively Brilliant Self-Mastery*, and creator of the Inspired Learning Model™

"Alan Seale's new book provides practical exercises and understanding for the spiritual seeker to engage with the soul and emerge as a transformational presence in the world."

—Richard Barrett, author of *The New Leadership Paradigm* and *Liberating the Corporate Soul*

"Going beyond conventional exercises, Seale offers depth and richness in a variety of customized practices that serve as stepping-stones along the journey of creating a life and a world that works."

—Maria Gamb, author of *Healing the Corporate World*

"Taking Alan Seale to heart opens vast new possibilities in a world that desperately needs transforming."

—A. Harris Stone, EdD, chancellor, the Graduate Institute

"I recommend Alan Seale's work to anyone who feels the inner drive to become more authentic and to help create a better future."

—Cindy Wigglesworth, president, Deep Change, Inc.

". . . filled with practical and transformative tools for the professional coach or anyone who truly wants to make a significant difference in our world."

—Stephanie Marisca, PCC, CTPC, professional coach, mentor, and trainer

"Thank you, Alan Seale, for investing the thought, effort, and discipline to provide this opportunity for partnering with the emerging potential in our world."

—Helle Nørlev, facilitator, IAF Denmark

"The connection Alan Seale makes between the self and the self within the world or the community is what is so needed today. Transforming the self and the world is the most empowering journey we can take to truly make a difference."

—Bronwyn Bowery-Ireland, CEO, International Coach Academy

Create
A World
That Works

TOOLS FOR PERSONAL
& GLOBAL TRANSFORMATION

ALAN SEALE

WEISERBOOKS
San Francisco, CA / Newburyport, MA

First published in 2011 by Red Wheel/Weiser, LLC
665 Third Street, Suite 400
San Francisco, CA 94107
www.redwheelweiser.com

Library of Congress Cataloging-in-Publication Data
Seale, Alan.
 Create a world that works : tools for personal and global transformation /
Alan Seale.
    p. cm.
Includes bibliographical references.
ISBN 978-1-57863-497-2 (alk. paper)
 1. Change (Psychology) 2. Self-realization. 3. Self-actualization
(Psychology) I. Title.
BF637.C4S43 2011
158.1—dc22
                        2011003638

Cover design by Jim Warner
Interior design by Stewart A. Williams
Typeset in Janson
Cover image © Prisma / SuperStock

Printed in Canada
TCP
10 9 8 7 6 5 4 3 2 1

The paper used in this publication meets the minimum requirements of the American National Standard for Information Sciences—Permanence of Paper for Printed Library Materials Z39.48-1992 (R1997).

To Devin Wilson

To be present is an act of creation.

Your presence—
how you show up to life—
no matter how powerful or subtle,
impacts what happens in your world,
just because you are there.

How do you choose to show up?
How do you choose to engage with the world?
How do you choose to make a difference?
How will you help create a world that works?

Contents

CREATING NEW REALITIES

FROM VERTICAL TO HORIZONTAL: TRANSFORMATIONAL PRESENCE IN ACTION

FOREWORD

Tools for Personal and Global Transformation

"What would you attempt to do if you knew you could not fail?" That's not only the question that I pose to myself, it's also the Robert Schuller quote that adorns my office wall as graffiti art and the sleek silver paperweight on my kitchen table. It's my internal monologue that prepares me for each day and challenges me for every tomorrow. It has been that persistent whisper that escalated to a scream until I was finally prepared to listen.

There is a unique path laid out for each of us, yet it is not certain that we will complete nor even begin this journey of self-understanding and fulfillment. My particular road map laid out three important lessons that took many years to explore and embrace, and I think they may be of some use to the readers of this important book. First, *you* are enough. And not only are you enough, you are an abundance, if you have the courage to embrace your unique gifts and talents and are not afraid to unleash them on the world. Second, failure is not a dirty word, a socially unacceptable outcome that has to be talked about in hushed tones. Reaching for something that seems so improbable, and may be, but means everything to you, is the very definition of opportunity—and the lifeblood of great social change movements. Finally, failure is ultimately nothing more than a state of mind—your state of mind. It's so easy to fall prey to doubts and fears. By building a community around you that will love you, stand for you, and be your fiercest champion, you will find opportunity in every two steps forward and one step back.

Each of us has a threshold, a turning point when the way we are living doesn't work anymore. The ultimate choice then becomes: do you continue with the way things are, or do you change? For me, this shift happened when overwhelming loss forced me to redefine my relationship to the world. For Alan Seale, during a lovely afternoon in France, he truly embraced his soul's call to once and for all claim and live his own powerful magnificence, wisdom, and awareness as never before. On this expedition, at that moment of obligation, there can be no turning back, no more gap between what you know and how you live.

With every fiber of my being, I believe that our core identity— who we truly are and what we are meant to do in this world—is as intrinsic as our DNA. Yet, for most of us, our very reason for being remains as invisible to us as those molecular building blocks because of self-imposed limitations, societal expectations, and just the relentless stuff of life. But it's there. It is etched in our soul, and it is ultimately our job to figure out what it is.

Create A World That Works: Tools for Personal and Global Transformation is your travel guide in becoming a Transformational Presence— someone who lives in an attitude of discovery, accesses potential, and learns from the future. In the subsequent pages, Alan discusses three big concepts: the Four Levels of Engagement, the Vertical and Horizontal Planes of Awareness, and the Potential-Based Approach. Through exploration of and inquiry into Transformational Presence, you will be able to implement these models of deep consciousness.

For most of the past two decades, I have had the great privilege of working with and learning from some of the world's most impactful social change agents. These social entrepreneurs are pioneers of innovations that benefit humanity, pragmatic visionaries with innovative solutions to society's most intractable problems. They matter to all of us, in part, because of their narrative power, the importance of their public example as societal catalysts. Historian Doris Kearns Goodwin once noted that it is the magic of leadership that allows a leader's example to reach down to people's self-definition and change it. Bottom line, these individuals walk the walk of Transformational Presence.

They embody and personify the power of individuals to get involved and make a difference.

In watching closely how these societal change agents walk through the world, I am fascinated by how aligned their makeup and actions are with Alan Seale's transformational framework. Whether they are tackling gender inequality in the largest slum in Africa, leveraging the capital markets to promote business opportunities for poor shopkeepers in Latin America, or confronting the achievement gap in America's classrooms, these visionaries exhibit a worldview, a sense of purpose, a focus on impact and power source that propels them each day to ever greater levels of awareness and action. They answer through their very being the questions infused throughout *Create A World That Works*: How do you choose to show up? What is my relationship to change? What if . . . ?

As you begin your process of transformation, please remember that while not common, transformation is ubiquitous. It happens throughout the universe in beautiful and profound ways. One of my favorite examples is courtesy of biologist Elisabet Sahtouris. Dr. Sahtouris studied the metamorphosis of a caterpillar into a butterfly. In metamorphosis, small cells called imaginal discs begin to appear in the body of the caterpillar. Since they're not recognized by the caterpillar's immune system, they are immediately wiped out. But as they grow in number and begin to link up, they ultimately overwhelm the caterpillar's immune system. Its body then goes into meltdown, and the imaginal discs build the butterfly from the spent materials of the caterpillar. This process is a natural articulation of what is possible when we let go of what no longer serves us and once and for all embrace our emerging potential.

Our future and our world demand no less. For as truly global citizens settling into the twenty-first century, we now find ourselves living and operating in turbulent and challenging yet interesting times. Old models of consumption, allocation, and expenditure no longer pass muster; new sustainable models for living are sorely needed. Fortunately, social entrepreneurs and other visionary leaders are in the vanguard of this new way of being. As Seale rightly points out, the future belongs to those who are creative, innovative, and original. He is speaking to you and inviting you into a sacred space. I'm so happy that you have accepted his invitation and committed yourself to this process of exploration and engagement. Shift happens because you make it so.

CHERYL L. DORSEY
President, Echoing Green

ACKNOWLEDGMENTS

Each of my books has brought its own process of creation and discovery, learning and development, and has been a gift to me in its own way. Yet somehow this book feels different. It feels as though I had to take the journey with all of the others in order to be able to write this one. So first, I am grateful for this extraordinary journey of life. Not a day goes by that I don't learn something new, understand something more deeply, or experience being touched by life's richness.

To Devin Wilson, thank you for your part in the creation of this book. It was through our deep conversations, rewarding friendship, and partnership in designing and leading the *Future World Now* program several years ago that this book found its beginnings. In the end, I was the one who wrote the book, but your spirit and energy have been very present throughout the process. It is with great joy that I dedicate this book to you.

Many thanks also to David Robinson, my dear friend and coleader in the Transformational Presence Coach Training program. Our rich conversations have helped open these concepts even further for me. Your insights and discoveries in working with the material added immeasurably to this book. Thank you for the gift of your presence in my life.

Thank you to all of the participants in both the Transformational Presence Coach Training program and in *Future World Now*. Your discoveries, insights, and experiences with this material were a great help to me in writing the book and in finding the right language for explaining big concepts.

Many thanks to Gabriella van Rooij, Marie Josee Smulders, Jos Rovers, Thom Schouten, Anna-Lena Smith, and Bercedeh Stark for their love and commitment to sharing this work in Europe. Thanks also to Daniel Karslake, Janet Dwinells, and Valerie Keller for their invaluable assistance in making connections.

Thanks to my publisher, Jan Johnson, for your continued belief in my work and your steadfast commitment to publishing books that foster transformation and healing in the world. And many thanks to the entire team at Red Wheel/Weiser for helping bring this book to the world.

Enormous thanks to my partner, Johnathon Pape, for being a valuable sounding board for ideas and for your early editing of the manuscript. Thank you for your great love and your participation in and support for all of my work. I am so blessed to have you in my life.

A heart full of love to my father, Rev. Dr. James Seale, who was always eager to read every article and manuscript and talk about big ideas and concepts. He crossed back to spirit just as this book was being completed. Yet his love of life, thirst for learning and growth, and commitment to realizing potential on every level live on in me and in these pages. Through his ministry, support and encouragement of others, and generous heart, he made a significant difference in more people's lives than we will ever know. His life and work remain an inspiration to me in my walk in the world.

Finally, to all of you who read this book and embody its principles, thank you for all you are and all you do to create a world that works.

Creating a Context

Instead of looking for heroic leaders to save us, each of us needs to be a hero or heroine. The call today asks for courageous and authentic people to connect with one another, to convene others, and . . . to bring form to the creative potential of the times in which we live.

—TOM HEUERMAN, PH.D., *leadership consultant*

We live in a time that calls us to claim responsibility for our lives and the creation of our world in ways never witnessed before. If we are to thrive as a human race, we must chart a new course. We must seriously consider what it would take to create a world that works. What would that world look like? How would life in that world be different? If we are the bridge between all that has been in human history and all that is yet to be created, what kind of bridge are we?

Few would argue that these times are tumultuous. Yet these times can also be transformational. Everything that we are, do, create, and think influences our present and future. How we approach our current circumstances—whether we focus on solving problems or creating a new world, whether we give energy to old paradigms or live in emerging potential—will determine what we create going forward. The choices and decisions are ours to make. The future is ours to create.

Those of us called to make a difference must be clear and intentional about how we "show up" to life. Regardless of whether we feel called to make a difference locally or globally, these times demand that we know and understand the power of authentic personal presence, understand life as energy in motion, and embody a personal presence that calls forth transformation in both ourselves and in the world around us. Indeed, our presence itself must become transformational.

Being a **Transformational Presence** means that we live in an attitude of discovery, access potential, learn from the future, and close the gap between what we know and how we live. Transformational Presence is rooted in expanding conscious awareness and inviting others into that space simply by being who we are. It is a way of living, leading, and serving that is built on cocreation and enlightened action. My purpose in writing this book is to offer, first, practical tools for developing Transformational Presence and, second, tools for envisioning and creating a world that works. These tools and concepts are not yet in the mainstream consciousness, but they are emerging on the periphery. They just need stewards to help them cross the bridge from concept to form.

Transformational Presence work means developing our greatest potential and the vast potential in everyone with whom we work. That development begins by tapping into soul—individual human souls, the collective soul of humanity, the souls of our communities and nations, the souls of our businesses and governments, the soul of the earth itself, and even the soul of the universe.

Transformational Presence calls us to get in touch with the authentic essence of life—an evolutionary intelligence, if you will—and let it guide us. Transformational Presence work starts with paying attention to the callings of our souls and the emerging potential in our world and having the courage to respond.

The word *soul* is showing up everywhere now—in advertising and branding, in literature, in numerous and diverse spiritual contexts. Its proliferation in our mainstream vocabulary reflects a huge spiritual hunger on every level of our society, a yearning for meaning and a connection with something bigger than ourselves. However, our culture hasn't been willing to fully address that yearning. Instead, it prefers buying its spirituality ready-made, adopting the latest fad, or taking a crash course in enlightenment. This desire for quick-and-easy spirituality is also evident in the rise of fundamentalist religious and/or spiritual beliefs that tell followers exactly what to do, think, and believe so that individuals don't have to sort things out for themselves.

Neither the spiritual fast food of popular culture nor the force-fed fundamentalist ideology (in any guise) is truly nourishing and empowering for individuals or the overall culture. In fact, both create a culture that does not think, feel deeply, or engage from the soul. Spiritual fast food engages and soothes the ego by letting it *think* it is doing something soulful. Fundamentalist beliefs at either end of the conservative-liberal spectrum engage our fear and judgment; dictate hard, fast, and inflexible "truths"; and leave no room for another opinion. Both keep us distanced from any true sense of responsibility for the creation of our world and from finding a center point that can truly serve a greater good.

What we need is *sustainable* soul food that nourishes and supports us at every level of our lives. We need people who live and lead from the soul, as well as from a sense of presence and grounding within the greater whole. We need people who are skilled at seeing both the big-picture view and the close-up detail at the same time. We need people who are willing to commit to visions and creations that may not, in fact, be fully realized in their lifetimes. We need people who are able to transcend the boundaries of personal, political, religious, and philosophical belief systems to find the places where we all can agree to meet. We need people who understand the power of Transformational Presence and are committed to developing their own Transformational Presence to its greatest potential.

It is time for each of us to claim our individual responsibility for the realities of our present and the unfolding course of our future. Some will lead their lives quietly and unnoticed, yet will still impact their community, region, and world with their choices and presence. Others will stand in front of the public by leading businesses, holding government offices, or becoming leaders of movements. No matter where we live and work, we have an unprecedented opportunity to participate in the evolution and advancement of our global civilization. Through leadership and service at whatever level, we can help people tap into the greatest potential of themselves, their companies, their families, their countries, and the world, and live that potential for the greater good of all. Transformational Presence work is another next step in the evolution of leadership and service.

In his book *Synchronicity*, Joseph Jaworski wrote:

> True leadership is about creating a domain in which we continually learn and become more capable of participating in our unfolding future. A true leader thus sets the stage on which predictable miracles, synchronistic in nature, can—and do—occur.
>
> The capacity to discover and participate in our unfolding future has more to do with our being—our total orientation of character and consciousness—than what we do. Leadership is about creating, day by day, a domain in which we and those around us continually deepen our understanding of reality and are able to participate in shaping the future. This, then, is the deeper territory of leadership—collectively "listening" to what is wanting to emerge in the world, and then having the courage to do what is required (p. 182).

Jaworski is speaking of leadership as cocreation with potential. Transformational Presence invites us to discover new levels and practices of cocreation. In the past, we might have thought of cocreation as a creative process between two or more people. Yet these times invite us to expand our concept of cocreation to include partnering with an idea or a potential to create something new. Everything that comes to us—whether it is a feeling, a comment, a circumstance, a challenge, or an outcome—is an opportunity for cocreation. Everything, whether or not we thought we wanted it, offers an opportunity to choose what we wish to create. Therefore, our first questions in any situation or circumstance must be, "What is the opportunity here? How can I accept this opportunity and work/play/create with it rather than resist it?"

One of the rules of improvisation, in theater or music, is that all participants must accept everything that is given to them from their fellow actors or musicians and continue to create from there. If one of the players refuses what is given to her, the whole performance becomes awkward and disjointed, and it is at risk of completely falling apart. In a similar way, martial arts use this principle. As your opponent comes at you in attack, you accept his or her energy and transform it through your body into personal strength and power.

When we adopt the same rules for life, we become empowered by everything that happens around us. We take whatever comes and work with it. It's not about liking or disliking or passing judgment on what comes to you. It's about being completely neutral to whatever comes and accepting it as a starting point from which to create, transform, and discover. When you embrace rather than push away, you can transform the energy of the situation. From there, you can usually find a way to move forward. However, if you refuse or form quick judgments on what comes, you are likely to miss the opportunities.

The fundamental principle of the universe is that everything is made up of vibrating energy. Energy cannot be created or destroyed—it can only be transformed. Cocreation is all about partnering with the energy and potential that is present and choosing how you wish to work with it—either in its present state or by transforming it to something else. This expanded understanding of cocreation is essential for transformational leadership and service. And it is essential for creating a world that works.

From where we stand today as a global civilization, creating a world that works is a complex and complicated undertaking. Even coming up with a picture of what that world would look like in the most basic and practical terms can be challenging. However, several characteristics come to mind. First, when I speak of a world that works, I do not mean to imply a perfect world. Our civilization is made up of billions of individuals, each of whom is on his or her own learning path. At times on that path, the learning curve gets pretty steep, both for individuals and for the collective. In a world that works, we acknowledge the challenges that come with learning, growth, and development and stand committed to working *with* one another instead of against one another.

To that end, in a world that works, people talk with one another, and perhaps even more importantly, they listen to one another. There is open communication between cultures, governments, and businesses. There is a willingness to hear and consider different ideas, approaches, value systems, and ways of thinking, and there is an understanding that no one has the whole truth. Seeing the entire picture of a particular issue requires seeing the perspectives of everyone involved. In those dialogues, sometimes it is easy to find the common goal and a path that everyone can agree on. At other times, there is disagreement and conflict. The many cultures of the world hold vastly different value structures and are in different places in their own evolution. Therefore, each culture is learning different lessons and working out different issues at different times.

In a world that works, there is a common understanding that everything is connected and that, therefore, everything impacts everything else. The well-being of one is ultimately dependent on the well-being of all. Therefore, there is a shared commitment to finding the path where everyone is served, where everyone gets something, where no choices or decisions are made to serve one at the expense of others.

In a world that works, people are willing to think *and* feel. They are willing to feel both pain and joy in themselves and others. They take personal, business, and government integrity seriously and accept responsibility for all their choices and actions, both those that turned out well and those that they regret. They are willing to recognize which choices and actions served a greater good and which ones served only a select few, and, as they go forward, to respond with choices that will serve every stakeholder.

In a world that works, there is also a common understanding that everything will not change overnight. In fact, some changes may take many years, even many generations, to be accomplished. Consider the beautiful cathedrals of Europe or many of the ancient temples and sanctuaries of the world. Many of them took more than a hundred years to build. Those who were a part of the project at the beginning of construction did not expect to see the completed building. The many artisans and craftsmen just focused on doing their part in the creation of something much larger—a project that would go on for many years to come. They took great pride in their work and in their contribution to the realization of a bigger vision. In a world that works, it is understood that some projects will be completed within months or a few years, while others will take much longer. People live in service of a greater good and a longer vision than might be realized in their individual lifetimes. In a world that works, cathedral building is considered part of the natural flow of creation and evolution within our human civilization.

These few characteristics of a world that works are only a beginning. As you read on, I invite you to start creating your own vision of a world that works, and watch that vision evolve as you experience this book's concepts and principles.

My aim throughout all my work has always been to integrate theory and practice, placing greater emphasis on the practice. The same is true for this book. My intention is to present just enough theory to ground the principles and concepts and then move into personal experience, understanding, and practical daily application in leadership and service. You will find "Inquiries" and "Explorations" in each chapter to help you delve deeper into the meaning of these concepts and tools for yourself. The Inquiries offer questions to help you more fully understand the relationship of a concept or principle to your daily life and work. The Explorations are experiential exercises to deepen your understanding and increase your ability to work with concepts and tools. I encourage you to take time for these Inquiries and Explorations. They are the bridges between understanding an idea and transformative action. You can also find audio versions of these Explorations at *www.transformationalpresence.org.*

Let's talk a little more about the comprehension and integration of big concepts. Yasuhiko Genku Kimura, author of *Think Kosmically, Act Globally*, wrote:

> Thinking for most people is *information-shuffling.* When they say they are thinking, they are in fact shuffling information.

True thinking is not shuffling information. The Japanese word for "to think" is "kamgaeru," which etymologically means "to return to the realm of God." The English word "to think" etymologically means "to make something appear" or "to create." To think thus etymologically means "to create by returning to the realm of God." Taking it a step further, to *think* means to *create in accord with the kosmic.* To create in accord with the kosmic means to bring forth new identities (concepts and ideas) by discovering new causative patterns through the unfolding of the knowledge of kosmic law or pattern integrity (p. 6).

Kimura invites us to take "thinking" beyond intellectual process—to return to the realm of the larger intuitive mind. Intellect is just one small part of your much more expansive intuitive mind. However, it is through the intellect that concepts are applied to daily living. The phrase "you need to get out of your head" implies that you should stop thinking with the intellect; yet doing so undermines the process of understanding and integrating new concepts into your life. Therefore, I invite you to *expand beyond* the intellect, not leave it behind. I invite you to think intuitively. Your intellect can then still be very present within your newly expanded awareness as the connection between that awareness and your daily life.

This intuitive thinking is a sharp contrast to how we are conditioned to approach life; our Western educational processes teach us to engage the intellectual mind and give little attention to the intuitive mind. However, engaging the intuitive mind is an essential part of transformational leadership and service. So I encourage you to allow your entry point for this book to be through your intuitive mind and then let this larger mind engage the intellect where appropriate. Chapters 5 through 10 will help you become more comfortable and facile with your intuitive mind.

I also invite you—and, in turn, those you serve—to take intuitive thinking a step further by consciously expanding beyond who you know yourself to be, the knowledge and understanding you have, and the structures that create and support your life. Again, I didn't say to toss them out! Simply expand beyond your present relationship to them. The future belongs to those who are creative, innovative, and original, and at the same time have the ability to walk away from their creations when they become obsolete, forging ahead into the next new creation. Expand beyond what you have created and what you have been taught. Staying within the boundaries of present understanding limits the potential of your experience. As you expand, who you are, what you know, and the structures that support you will all remain in place. The difference is that by expanding beyond intellect, you can let go of your hold on, dependence on, or attachment to those identities and structures so that you are free to grow into a new way of living. As you grow, you will also attract new structures that support your new awareness and understanding.

Finally, I invite you to become a coexplorer of these ideas and concepts with me. I don't consider myself to be the creator of this material, but a steward for it. I've been lucky enough to become aware of this evolutionary movement that is sweeping the globe and to invite some of it to "sweep" through me. You can do the same. So let these pages be part teacher, part cocreator, part mentor, part catalyst—whatever they may be in any particular moment. The result can be greater clarity and understanding, for you and those you serve, about how to envision and create a world that works.

And so we begin.

CHAPTER ONE

The Anatomy of Transformational Presence

The way of the Creative works through change and transformation, so that each thing receives its true nature and destiny
and comes into permanent accord with the Great Harmony;
this is what furthers and what perseveres.

—ALEXANDER POPE, *English poet*

Presence is the energy essence that you radiate or emanate, either
as an individual or a collective, simply by being who you are. Presence is made up of who you are at your essence plus your thoughts,
beliefs, attitudes, intentions, and behaviors. It is how you show up in
the world, the energetic space that your being creates, and the energy
that you bring to challenges, opportunities, dreams, and visions.

Transformation is a shift from one state of being to another. It happens at the vibrational or quantum level. Therefore, transformation
occurs fundamentally as a result of a shift in vibrational frequency.
In an individual, transformation means the whole of his or her being
and consciousness shifts to vibrate at a new frequency. In the same
way, organizational or societal transformation means that the whole
of the organization or society—its members, culture, beliefs, and
practices—is now sourced from a different vibrational frequency.

Any sustainable difference in our world is rooted in transformation of
some kind—transformation of being, understanding, and, ultimately, of
practice. Transformational leadership and service involves creating the

energetic space that supports vibrational shifts in being and consciousness, ultimately leading to significant shifts in practices, choices, decisions, and actions. When positive transformation occurs, whether for an individual, organization, or society, their presence—how they show up in the world—becomes more powerful and impactful in some way.

Transformational Presence is a result of a state of being in which you live, work, and engage in life from a place of profound alignment—alignment between your soul, its mission or reason for being, greater Consciousness, and the greater potential waiting to emerge in any moment—and of a dynamic balance between power and love. Martin Luther King Jr., quoted in James Washington's *A Testament of Hope: The Essential Writings of Martin Luther King, Jr.*, articulated this balance:

> Power, properly understood, is nothing but the ability to achieve purpose . . . There is nothing wrong with power if power is used correctly . . . One of the great problems of history is that the concepts of love and power have usually been contrasted as opposites—polar opposites—so that love is identified with a resignation of power, and power with a denial of love. . . . What is needed is a realization that power without love is reckless and abusive, and love without power is sentimental and anemic. (pp. 246-47)

Presence: how an individual or organization "shows up" in the world, the energetic space that their "being" creates, and the energy that they bring to challenges, opportunities, dreams, and visions.

Transformational Presence: a state of being in which one lives, leads, works, and engages in life from a place of profound alignment with one's soul, one's soul mission or life purpose, and the greater Consciousness. This presence opens the door to the greater potential waiting to emerge in any moment, situation, or circumstance, and to becoming a steward for that potential to manifest.

When this alignment and balance are in place, you become an embodiment of evolutionary intelligence in action. You emanate an authentically powerful presence that creates an energetic space in which transformation is likely to occur. This presence opens the door to the greater potential waiting to emerge in any moment, situation, or circumstance and to becoming a steward for that potential to manifest. The more authentic and dynamic an individual or organization's presence, the more effectively that individual or organization serves the positive transformation and evolution of our world.

Transformational Presence is a result of a profound sense of oneness with Consciousness. By Consciousness I mean the matrix of energy that is the creative and sustaining force of all that is. You could also call it God, Spirit, Intelligence, Great Mystery, the Force, or some other term. I use the word *Consciousness* in this book because of its universal nature. Please substitute whatever term works best for you. I also make a distinction between *Consciousness* and *consciousness*, capitalized and not. By *Consciousness*, I mean the creative and sustaining force of all; I use *consciousness* to refer to the awareness and fundamental state of being of a group, organization, or culture.

A profound sense of oneness with Consciousness does not mean that we as individuals *are* greater Consciousness, but rather that we are held within it and are human manifestations of *aspects of* greater Consciousness. We contain within us *the essence* of greater Consciousness. Our presence becomes transformational as we grow in understanding of how Consciousness works (at least as much as is possible), as we align our lives with our soul essence, and as we enter into dynamic, cocreative partnership with the evolutionary intelligence propelling us forward as a human civilization in a more than human world.

When you show up to life, leadership, and service as an embodiment of Transformational Presence, you can be much more effective in facilitating quantum shifts within those around you and those you serve. As a result, *they* begin showing up in the world in more effective, productive, inspiring, and empowering ways. Through helping those you serve understand how they made those shifts and how life works as energy in motion, as well as helping them learn to partner with potential, you empower them to impact *their* worlds in profound ways.

No one can make these shifts happen in us, nor can we make them happen in anyone else. Each person must ultimately do that for him- or herself by being fully present to the moment and its potential and allowing shifts to occur. However, embodying Transformational Presence creates and holds the optimal space for transformation in others and circumstances to happen. A part of what makes one's presence transformational is holding clear and focused intention and creating the optimal conditions for another's greatness to come through. Transformational Presence means being in an open, creative, and intuitively perceptive space so that you can ask the questions and open the doors that will allow those you serve to experience and embrace the shifts that are ready to occur. Transformational Presence means holding a space for discovery, opening wide the doors and windows of the mind and spirit for ever-expanding awareness and understanding, ever-deepening knowledge and wisdom. This discovery can ultimately lead to more productive and sustainable actions and outcomes. From inner transformation comes sustainable outer change of circumstances and ways of living and working. As we call forth the greatness in others and support their personal transformation, they, in turn, learn to do the same for those in their sphere of influence.

While leadership and service certainly can include helping others with the mechanics of how things are done, with best practices, and with specific job-related skills, the primary focus of this book is to help you become a more authentic and powerful presence in all that you do. Through this presence, you are then able to support those you serve in achieving deeper self-discovery, recognizing who they are at their essence, and making clear choices about how they choose to show up in the many aspects of their lives. You are able to support them in developing *their* Transformational Presence, understanding their role in creating a world that works, and implementing plans of action. My intention is to give you a greater understanding of how life works as energy in motion and to help you discover how to partner with energy and potential for accelerated and often extraordinary results. As you integrate that knowledge and understanding in your life and work to the point where it becomes the way you live—your default approach to thinking, perceiving, making decisions, and taking action—you begin to emanate Transformational Presence.

The concepts of Transformational Presence can serve as a foundation for all forms of leadership and service—indeed, for anyone committed to making a difference in their world. Making a difference begins with calling forth the human spirit. It is through the human spirit that the breath of Consciousness moves through each of us. Within this fundamental context, we explore goals, challenges, visions, and dreams with those we serve, regardless of whether we are working in organizations, business, government, or personal development.

Transformational work includes helping people and organizations understand that they have choices in how they meet the world every day—choices about who they are and who they will be; choices about how they will respond to situations, challenges, opportunities, and circumstances; choices about the decisions they make, actions they take, and kinds of relationships they engage in. We help them discover, on a multitude of levels, that while they may not be able to change their circumstances right away, they *can* choose who they will be in relation to those circumstances. And they can make choices and move into action in proactive ways to support the transformational shifts that are trying to happen.

Helping people and organizations understand that they have choices about everything, even when they think they don't, is one of the most important gifts that we can give to the world. From there, we can help them tap into the essence of their being, their soul, and support them in making choices and decisions that not only move them forward, but also contribute to forward movement of a greater good. Every choice, thought, decision, action, and opinion instantly impacts our present-day mass consciousness and contributes to the shaping of the consciousness into which future generations will be born. When we develop our own, individual Transformational Presence, we then have the opportunity to help open our present-day mass consciousness to a more expansive, inclusive, and compassionate way of being with one another. In this way, we truly create a better world for our grandchildren's children to be born into.

There are many qualities that go together to create a Transformational Presence. However, five qualities provide the building blocks for all the rest. The first is deep self-awareness at the soul level. You must know who you are at your essence, what is important to you, what makes you tick. You must be aware of when something works well for you and allows you to be your best in the world, as well as when something is not right for you. This does not mean that you must have reached enlightenment or self-mastery. It means that you have developed your awareness to the point that you know yourself very well and that you are aware of what is going on in your inner world. If you are going to call forth and support others in their own deep self-awareness, you must be comfortable with that process within yourself.

The second quality is living your life in a way that is congruent with your essence. Your choices, decisions, and actions must resonate in harmony with your soul. Again, this doesn't mean that you never again make a decision or act in a way that you later regret. It means that you learn from those experiences and take steps to bring your choices and actions into alignment with your soul as soon as you realize that something is incongruent.

The third quality is intuitive thinking—engaging the intuitive mind in daily life and work. We have already defined the intuitive mind as the greater mind, of which intellect is only a small part. When you engage the intuitive mind, you have access to a much greater world of information, wisdom, creativity, and innovation. Intuitive intelligence encompasses all of your intelligences—intellectual, emotional, spiritual, social—and opens the door to greater understanding and more effective interaction with your world.

The fourth quality is a clear understanding, at both an intuitive and intellectual level, of the laws of energy. This understanding allows you to connect the knowledge, wisdom, and understanding of ancient wisdom traditions with quantum energy concepts. That connection brings a greater understanding of what it means to align thoughts, beliefs, intentions, actions, and habits with soul and soul mission.

When you understand these concepts both intuitively and intellectu-ally, you are better equipped to speak about and implement them in a mainstream world. Bringing you this understanding is a large part of what this book is about.

Finally, those with the most powerful Transformational Presence have some form of daily reflective practice. People often ask me what form of practice I recommend, and my response is always, "Whatever works!" What is important is not so much the form, but rather that you have a daily practice of some kind that works for you. The only qualification I make is that silence be kept during at least a part of the practice. For you, this practice may take the form of meditation, prayer, journaling, running, walking in nature, or doing yoga or martial arts. The key is that you have a daily time set aside for reflection, introspection, and connec-tion with your soul and whatever you may call the creative and sustain-ing force of all that is. It is through introspective and reflective practice that you develop your mentoring relationship with Consciousness. And it is through your ongoing practice in the silence over time that you discover the rock-solid foundation within you—beliefs and deep under-standing—that can support you regardless of the challenges that arise.

Transformational Presence includes exploring ideas, beliefs, and concepts without judgment. It requires listening on many levels of awareness—listening for the voice of the soul, for the words under-neath the words, listening for the essence of what is happening and the gift that is waiting to be opened or the opportunity that is waiting to unfold. Transformational Presence means listening from a place of profound knowledge and understanding of the laws of energy and the nature of the soul. It means helping those we serve streamline their awareness so that they become masters at identifying and partner-ing with the potential that is waiting to unfold. We begin by learn-ing to do all of these things for ourselves. As we support others in their development, our learning continues to deepen, and we create a foundation of broader understanding and expanded awareness upon which to build a world that works.

Our journey together through this book is about helping you dis-cover, develop, and refine your personal sense of Transformational

Presence, and then helping you develop tools and skills for calling forth the unique and powerful presence of others. Indeed, our work is about calling forth greatness from everyone and every situation around us, first and foremost by how we show up in the moment.

Transformation involves letting that which no longer serves die. Death is itself transformation—a crossing from one state of being to another. If we are constantly growing and evolving, we are constantly dying and being born again to new awareness. In time, our current realities become too tight and hold us back from the possibilities and even greater potentials that await us. If we want to *keep* growing and evolving, we have to be willing to let go of beliefs, habits, roles, and practices when they become too tight. We must be willing to take off our current realities and step into new ones. We must let go of our perceptions of who we have been and step into the next generation of who we are called to be in the service of the larger evolutionary path of our communities, countries, and world.

We can easily say that anything is possible, yet we can also get lost in the vastness of possibility and potential. This book offers tools for clarifying and naming the "anything" that is now wanting to become reality through you, partnering with it, and bringing it into your three-dimensional reality. Transformational Presence is a way of being and perceiving that invites us and those we serve to more deeply and actively engage in and serve the evolution of the human race and of Consciousness itself in order to create a world that works. It involves exploring new frontiers of human beingness and what it means to recognize the greatest potential of the future and live it now. It calls us to partner with potential and Consciousness, to participate in the ongoing evolution of the collective consciousness and, therefore, in the creation of the world that future generations will inhabit.

We are the stewards of our present and future. We are the hands and feet of Consciousness and potential. We are the ones we have been waiting for. Creating a world that works begins with all of us standing tall in our own Transformational Presence.

FOUR LEVELS
OF ENGAGEMENT

CHAPTER TWO

Getting to the Essence

We are all faced with a series of great opportunities brilliantly disguised as impossible situations.

—CHARLES R. SWINDOLL, *American writer and clergyman*

We begin this journey with a simple model of how we engage with life. In a very general way, you could say that there are four levels of awareness from which we engage with our daily experiences: drama, situation, choice, and opportunity. I know that this suggestion dates me, but you can remember the four levels by the acronym *DSCO* (pronounced "disco").

In leadership and service, the Four Levels of Engagement give us a structure for getting to the true essence of what is going on as quickly as possible. In the same way, when we introduce this simple structure to those we serve, we give them an awareness tool that helps them begin to make significant shifts in how they approach challenges and situations. The simplicity of the model quickly expands awareness. Understanding these four levels is also a first step toward Transformational Presence and creating a world that works.

Drama lives at the surface. The Drama level of engagement is the "he said, she said, then this happened, and then she said, and then he said . . ." level. It is so easy to get caught up in that level and start *reacting* to the emotions of a situation or story before pausing to consider how we want to respond. Reacting can be a significant trap when we want to be sensitive to others' needs, feelings, and circumstances. Even for those who are more experienced in leadership and service, some people and situations can easily pull you in, especially if you have an emotional stake in what is going on.

At the Drama level, the focus is usually on finding someone to blame. Typical questions are, "Whose fault is this? How did this happen? Can you believe he did that? What were they thinking?" Bring to mind a time when you have gotten caught in the Drama level in your personal or professional life. How did that feel? What happened to your focus and energy? Going to the Drama level can happen to any of us; you are not alone! Yet with heightened awareness and practice, you can learn to quickly drop beneath the drama and begin to perceive and understand more clearly. As you keep practicing, you get caught in the Drama level much less frequently.

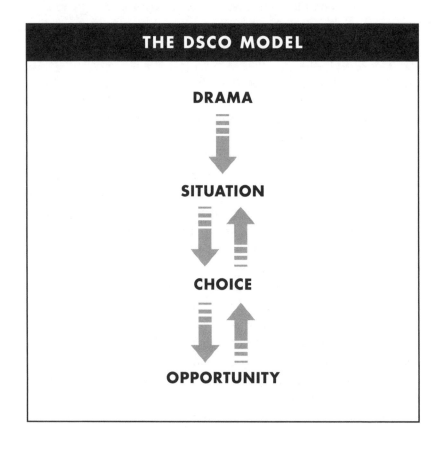

THE DSCO MODEL

DRAMA

SITUATION

CHOICE

OPPORTUNITY

As we drop below Drama, we come to the Situation level. Because we've stepped beyond the drama, we are able to see what is going on much more clearly—what really happened or is happening. The typical question here is, "How do we fix it?" The main focus at the Situation level is usually damage control. How quickly can we fix the problem and get things back to "normal"? We move on and put the situation behind us, usually without learning from what has happened. As a result, a similar situation or challenge is likely to come up again, because the real underlying issues were never addressed. Unfortunately, too often this level is as far as we go. We are well trained to look for who or what to blame or to be problem solvers and remain in these first two levels.

The third level, Choice, invites us into a shift in consciousness. Here we are not speaking of choices about how to fix a situation, but choice about who we will be within the situation—our relationship to what is happening. At this level, the questions are, "Who am I within this situation? What is my role in how the situation came to be? What is my role in what is happening now? How do I choose to engage going forward?" This third level invites us to recognize that although we may not be able to change the circumstances or situation right away, we can at least choose who we will be within them. And that's a huge step beyond where most people go. Now we and those we serve are claiming responsibility and choice in the matter, and together we can start to create something new. The door is now open for the possibilities of transformation and sustainable change.

Finally, there is the fourth level, the deepest level, the one that we rarely get to in our culture, and the one where the most profound leadership and service occur: Opportunity. When we move to Opportunity, our first question becomes, "What's the opportunity here?" or "What wants to happen?" This level is where the true power lies. Here we get to the gold. This situation has happened for a reason. It wants to tell us something—to help us clearly recognize what is not working or what wants to change or heal. In fact, there is usually a direct correlation between the Drama and the Opportunity levels: the bigger the drama, the greater the opportunity. The drama is a wake-up call, alerting us that something wants to shift or transform.

Once we have identified the opportunity, we then choose how we want to engage with it and what role we will play. As we engage with the opportunity, we continue to move back and forth between the Choice and Opportunity levels. Each choice reveals more about the opportunity, and the deeper we go into the opportunity, the clearer our choices become. As a result, our perception of the situation starts to change, and we are able to move forward with new levels of insight and clarity.

When we live in Drama and Situation, life tends to be about struggle and problem solving. We give the power to something outside of us, and we reinforce the presence and action that keep us stuck. However, when we move to Choice and Opportunity, we take the power back. Consciously choosing who we will be in relationship to the situation empowers us to break free from struggle and create new circumstances and realities.

Leading and serving from the Opportunity level cuts to the chase. Asking, "What wants to happen?" invites everyone involved to a higher level of awareness. At this deeper level, there can be great learning

FOUR LEVELS OF ENGAGEMENT

LEVEL	TYPICAL QUESTIONS
Drama	Whose fault is this? Whom do I blame? Can you believe this happened?
Situation	How can we fix it, and how quickly?
Choice	Whom do I choose to be here? What do I choose as my relationship to this situation?
Opportunity	What's the opportunity here? What wants to happen?

and powerful forward movement for everyone involved. It opens the door to much greater insight and information than if we were to just fix the problem as fast as we can. And it certainly brings much greater awareness than is available while reacting at the Drama level!

Learning to live and work from the Choice and Opportunity levels starts with being focused and disciplined enough to step beyond the drama and then being courageous enough to name the opportunity rather than just solve a problem. It starts with being bold enough to *choose who you will be*, what relationship you will have to circumstances you meet, and to make a habit of asking, "What's the opportunity here?" In this way, you help those you serve come to the levels of Choice and Opportunity as well. You take the first step toward creating a world that works.

Transformational Presence means listening and responding from Choice and Opportunity regardless of where others are. The more you engage life from Choice and Opportunity, the more those you serve will learn to live at these deeper levels of awareness, to view situations from Choice and Opportunity, and to radiate a more powerful presence in their lives and work. Therefore, engaging life from the levels of Choice and Opportunity is the beginning of helping others stand in their own Transformational Presence.

Exploration: Four Levels of Engagement

Of the four levels—Drama, Situation, Choice, and Opportunity—at which one do you live most of the time? What is your default level?

Over the next few days, pay close attention to how you respond to situations and circumstances in your life—to challenges, conflicts, and opportunities. Do you tend to get caught up in or even create drama? Do you go straight to the Situation level and look for solutions as quickly as possible? Or do you pause to reflect and move quickly to Choice and Opportunity? Make no judgment about what you observe. Just pay attention and see what starts to shift in your awareness simply through noticing your default reactions.

In your leadership and/or service, notice to which levels those you serve automatically go. And notice then how you respond to them when they do. If they go to Drama or Situation, do you meet them there and stay at those levels, reacting to and fixing problems? Or do you acknowledge the challenge of their situation and then invite them to another level of awareness? From what level do you listen?

Once those you serve are in Choice or Opportunity, how can you help them explore their opportunities to the fullest and experience transformation on some level? How can you help them choose Choice and Opportunity all the time?

Creating a world that works begins with living at the Choice and Opportunity levels. "What wants to happen here?" becomes your mantra. From there, you keep listening on many levels of awareness, letting what wants to happen show you the way forward. Choosing to live at these levels is a simple yet profound shift in how you approach life, leadership, and service. It is the first layer of the foundation for Transformational Presence.

CHAPTER THREE

Once and for All

Until one is committed there is hesitancy, the chance to draw back, always ineffectiveness. Concerning all acts of initiative (and creation) there is one elementary truth, the ignorance of which kills countless ideas and splendid plans: the moment one definitely commits oneself, Providence moves too. All sorts of things occur to help one that would otherwise never have occurred. A whole stream of events issues from the decision, raising in one's favor all manner of unforeseen incidents and meetings and material assistance, which no man could have dreamed would have come his way.

—W. N. MURRAY, *author of*
The Scottish Himalayan Expedition

The more we live at the Choice and Opportunity levels of engagement, the more we become aware of breakthroughs necessary to living in the opportunities that reveal themselves. As transformers, part of our job is to notice breakthrough potential as it emerges and call ourselves and those we serve forward to the opportunity. Breakthroughs happen when we transform paradigms that no longer serve, methods that sustain the status quo, habits and beliefs that keep us and those with whom we work stuck in old patterns and ways of working and being. However, too often, we stop just short of the breakthrough actually happening.

Successful breakthroughs ask for "once and for all" commitments. This powerful commitment is perhaps best explained through my own experience. I discovered this simple yet profound concept at a 2004 gathering of coaches from around the globe in southern France. During an exercise on the afternoon of our second day together, I intuitively heard my soul ask, "Will you finally make this shift once and for all?"

The shift was to claim my own power and gifts on an entirely new level. I had experienced fleeting awareness of this level of power and being before. I had known for some time that it was there and available to me, and that claiming it was a major life lesson. I had been amazed by it, had stood in awe and wonder of it, had been fascinated by the idea of what life would be like if I lived there, and was committed to *continuing to move toward* living full-time in that new power and awareness. Yet I had never taken the simple but profound step of choosing to *live in that reality right now.* I had never stepped in once and for all and said, "There is no turning back." In that moment, I realized it was no longer good enough to hold an intention that someday I would get there. *I had to live it now.*

I answered the call with a resounding *yes!* It was a yes like I have never said before. There was an instantaneous energetic shift within me. I literally felt my whole system catapult to a much higher vibrational frequency. I had fleetingly experienced this frequency before, but I knew now in my core that this shift was permanent. It was a visceral knowing.

It has been many years since that transformational moment in France, yet I continue to experience a very high-frequency, humming vibration at my core, and it brings with it a more profound stillness, peace, trust, and knowingness than I had known before. And it is here to stay. I have no doubt. It has briefly faded from time to time, but as soon as I recall that moment in France and remind myself of my commitment, I'm right back on track. The shift was indeed once and for all.

That day, I realized that even though many of us have a lot of knowledge and possess tremendous awareness, there is often a significant gap between what we know and how we live. Bridging that gap takes us into *action of being*—action that comes directly out of *living* our wisdom, knowledge, and awareness, not just talking about it. Action of being means being grounded in soul awareness and following its guidance into action. On that afternoon in France, I was called by my soul to once and for all claim and live my own powerful magnificence, wisdom, and awareness as never before. No turning back. No more gap between what I knew and how I lived. I was called to create within my thought and belief the new reality in which I wished to live and to *live there now*, not just visit from time to time.

Does once and for all mean that you will never slip back into an old pattern, belief, or fear? Probably not. However, it does mean that you have now made a commitment to living from this new awareness and never again have to agonize over what your commitment is. Without commitment, life lacks energy and power. When you waver in your commitment, you may find yourself trying over and over again to sort out what is important to you, who you choose to be, what principles will guide your life. In that process, you can feel your energy and power draining away. Making the once-and-for-all commitment restores energy and power. From that point forward, if you slip back, you acknowledge the slip and immediately set yourself back on track. There is no more sitting on the fence, trying to decide what to do or whether or not to commit. No more energy drain. You have committed. It is done.

Once and for all is a powerful commitment not only to yourself, but also to the whole human family. On the personal level, "once and for all" means that you are committed to the shift and the transformation, and that is now the reality in which you live. However, achieving that shift is only the beginning. The commitment is once and for *all*—for everyone. "For all" means that as you experience transformation, you open the door or blaze the trail for others who are in a similar place or circumstance. Whether the transformation takes place at the personal or organizational level, you carve a pathway in consciousness. And as you walk down the path of transformation, you help to make the path clearer, wider, smoother, easier for others to find and follow.

Yet there is still more. The most profound aspect of my experience was the recognition that this permanent transformation came as a result of a choice—*my* choice to respond to the calling of my soul to claim my gifts and serve on a broader scale. When I heard the request of my soul, I chose to say yes. *It was that choice to say yes* that transformed my being, not an outside event or even the powerful support of the group. I had touched that new level of inner power before, but no transformation had occurred. It took the final step of *choosing* to be transformed once and for all.

Since making that choice, many doors have opened in my work. Opportunities for international collaborations began appearing immediately. I started receiving more invitations to teach and speak. My coaching practice blasted to a new level, and synchronicities increased exponentially.

Calling forth greatness means calling ourselves and those we serve to make once-and-for-all choices that, one after another, lead to living in service of a greater good. Creating a world that works requires embracing our own gifts and creating a space that supports the dynamic and complete unfolding of the greatest potential of individuals and opportunities alike. As we support others in realizing their greatest potential, their presence becomes transformational for others.

Intend and claim that with every step you take forward in life and in the development of your consciousness, you take that step for all. Invite those you serve to do the same. Ask how your current vision or goal is serving, empowering, calling forth the greatness of everyone whose lives it will touch. How is this growth a step forward for all?

When you have made a commitment and experienced the once and for all, you have taken a significant step in the journey of transformation. Now you must surrender to your commitment, letting it guide you, and discipline yourself to stay the course. What you are actually surrendering to is a greater presence of you. And the more you surrender to your greater presence, the more that presence becomes transformational.

As you continue to read and work with the concepts and principles in this book, be aware of the once and for alls that are wanting to happen—that are calling out to you and saying, "Now is the time! Do it!" Call the awareness of those you serve to these moments in their lives and work. These breakthrough commitments lead you to living your greatest potential. These commitments help you evolve into a person who emanates Transformational Presence and, in turn, help you support that evolution in others.

Inquiry: Once and for All

"Once and for all" is a conscious choice and commitment that can catapult you to new levels of awareness and action. It can open the door for others to step up to a new level as well. Consider the questions below. Then, after completing these inquiries for yourself, consider how you can use them in your work with others.

Find a place where you can enter into a calm, contemplative state of being. Once in that spot, ask yourself what breakthroughs are wanting to happen in your life. What choices and commitments are you being called to make now, once and for all? Perhaps the answers are clear to you right away. If not, perhaps one of these questions will bring more clarity:

➤ What have you been avoiding, such as a conversation that needs to be had or a habit that needs to be changed?
➤ What permanent shift needs to occur in your thinking; your approach to life, leadership, or service; your beliefs; or your presence in order for you to take the next step in your personal and/or organizational evolution?
➤ What do you know, but don't yet live?
➤ In what ways might your actions need to be more in alignment with your beliefs and values?

Once you find an area calling for a once-and-for-all commitment, take the step. Make the commitment. Then find a way to honor this powerful choice you are making. Write it down in your journal. Share it with a loved one. Perform a ritual. Do what you need to do to experience the transformation, and let that shift pour through you and out into the collective consciousness—once and for all. Make that transformation now, and you don't have to do it again. Claim that transformation and live it.

CHAPTER FOUR

Vertical and Horizontal Orientations of Awareness

When you do things from your soul,
you feel a river moving in you, a joy.
When actions come from another section,
the feeling disappears.

—RUMI, *Sufi mystic and poet*

Both leadership and service, in the most general sense, are processes of facilitating personal and/or organizational growth, change, development, and/or accomplishment. Our society measures success in those areas by quantifying visible and tangible results. While, in the end, tangible results are definitely important, in order for growth, change, development, and accomplishment to be lasting, sustainable, and systemic, transformation must occur at deep inner levels, and the results of transformation on those levels are not so easily quantifiable.

One of the most ancient symbols in human civilization is the cross. It has been found in cave wall carvings dating back to the Stone Age, as well as in the art and iconography of many cultures and spiritual traditions. While the basic cross has been used to represent many things, it is most commonly used to represent a union of the spiritual and material worlds, of heaven and earth. It has also been used to represent the human body; the four elements of air, fire, water, and earth; the four directions of east, south, west, and north; and the four seasons.

The cross is also a powerful metaphor for two fundamental

orientations to living: vertical and horizontal—who we *are* in the world and what we *do* in the world. The vertical plane of the cross represents *being*—who we, as individuals or organizations, are at our essence and the alignment of who we are with Consciousness. The horizontal orientation represents *doing*—action and accomplishment in the physical world. The diagram here illustrates the vertical and horizontal planes. Where they overlap in the center, where being and doing come together, is the area of our greatest impact and accomplishment. Being alone ultimately lacks effectiveness. Doing without being lacks meaning and insight, as well as a sense of a bigger picture. Therefore, neither is sustainable in daily life without the other. However, when both are fully engaged, great things can happen.

Our mainstream Western culture has been primarily focused on the horizontal plane. Value and worth have been measured by actions, accomplishments, skills, and productivity. Our culture offers very little support or instruction for tapping into the vertical. Self-awareness, intuitive awareness, and an ability to access both a bigger vision and the unseen world of energy and potential have not been a part of our educational processes or consciousness. However, the winds are shifting, and we are witnessing a gradual awakening to the importance of the vertical connection.

It is through the vertical plane that you get in touch with your soul and soul mission and bring all of the aspects of your being—your thoughts, beliefs, intentions, attitudes, perspectives—into alignment with that essence and mission. When this alignment is not in place, you may have a feeling of being out of sorts or out of touch with yourself, your place or role in situations, and even how you fit into your world. A sense of true and authentic confidence may be lacking. However, when you are in alignment within yourself, you experience a sense of being centered and grounded, a confident feeling of "having it together." The stronger and more secure this alignment is, the more you know who you are and why you are here. You recognize your gifts and the contributions you are here to make. You learn to trust your intuitive mind and recognize it as the greater mind, of which the intellect is only a small part.

Being

Doing   Impact

               Accomplishment   Doing

Being

Beyond personal alignment in the vertical plane comes alignment with the bigger picture of life—a sense of connection and alignment with the earth and the universe. (See the diagram here.) From the vertical plane, you are able to see the larger contexts within which the events of the horizontal plane are unfolding. Through the vertical plane, you can learn to sense the greater potential ready to emerge within your life, as well as the greater potential ready to emerge within a situation, project, or organization. You intuitively recognize what wants to happen. You can learn to partner with that potential and with greater Consciousness and be a steward for helping that potential become reality. You can learn to recognize what is wanting to happen in service of the greater good through your life and projects. And you can learn to see how your life and projects are a part of a much larger evolutionary flow. Through the vertical plane, you can learn to tap into Consciousness and let it guide you.

As you find that vertical alignment, you step into the horizontal plane and move into action. While work in the vertical plane is largely inner work and, therefore, often not recognized by others, moving to the horizontal plane takes you into the outer world—the world of structure and form, what the mainstream culture might call the real world.

When you are in the horizontal plane alone, with no connection to the vertical, your awareness is limited to the three-dimensional realm. You have no access to a bigger picture or a sense of energy and potential. You can easily feel like you are living in a world where you must push and shove to make things happen. Furthermore, while actions and projects reside in the horizontal plane, the meaning or personal connection and motivation for those actions reside in the vertical plane. When there is no personal meaning or connection between the project or goal and the people involved, the project is not likely to be sustainable. Sustainability requires meaning and connection. However, when your action in the horizontal plane is informed by intuitive awareness, insight, and alignment with the big-picture view of the vertical plane, and rooted in meaning and personal motivation, you can accomplish incredible things. Living and leading from the intersection of the vertical and horizontal produces the action of being that was introduced in the last chapter.

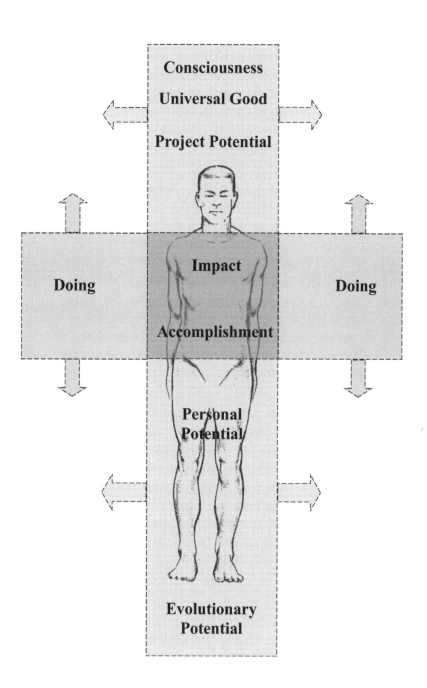

To a large degree, the greater the height and depth of awareness in the vertical plane, and the greater your alignment between all aspects of yourself, the emerging potential, and greater Consciousness, the greater your success and impact will be in the horizontal plane. Action of being begins with establishing the vertical alignment, and from there widening the vertical into the horizontal, so that every action in the horizontal plane is informed by the power, wisdom, and insight of the vertical. By widening the vertical, you also, in effect, expand to much greater height and depth in the horizontal, creating a much larger intersection between the vertical and horizontal and, therefore, a large sphere of energy, impact, and accomplishment—all informed by a great vertical alignment and awareness. (The diagram on page 27 illustrates this expansion.) Action of being occurs in the intersection between vertical and horizontal. Therefore, the wider the vertical expands into the horizontal, and the deeper and higher the horizontal expands into the vertical, the larger the intersection of the two planes becomes, and the greater your impact and accomplishment.

In the horizontal plane, the inspiration of the vertical plane turns into action. Through that action comes learning, which, in turn, inspires deeper understanding, exploration, discovery, and transformation in the vertical plane. That transformation then leads to new choices, actions, habits, and practices in the horizontal. In the dynamic balance between vertical and horizontal orientations of awareness, each plane continues to inform and inspire the other. Transformational Presence is, in part, a result of a dynamic and sustainable balance between these two planes.

The Four Levels of Engagement, explored in chapter 2, have a direct correlation to vertical and horizontal orientations of living. Drama and Situation exist primarily on the horizontal plane. Choice and Opportunity move us into the vertical plane to give clarity and insight into what is really going on from a big-picture perspective. From the vertical plane, you are able to see the larger context and who you are called to be, as well as the greater opportunities that are waiting to be discovered.

While we can talk about the vertical and horizontal planes at length, the best way to understand how they apply to our lives may be to experience them. The following exercise will show you your own experience of these planes of orientation.

Exploration: The Vertical and Horizontal Orientations of Awareness

Stand in an open space with your feet about shoulder width apart and parallel to one another. Extend your arms out from your shoulders, so that the trunk of your body becomes the vertical plane of being in the vertical-horizontal cross and your extended arms and hands become the horizontal plane of doing or action. Notice the relationship of your hands to your body and how it feels to stand in this position, with your body straight and arms and hands extended outward. Do your hands feel like they are an extension of your trunk and connected to your heart, or do they feel disconnected and separate? Are your arms energized and supported, or does it take effort to hold them up? You don't need to do anything with what you are feeling or try to change or adjust anything. Just notice.

Now gently drop your arms to your sides.

After a brief rest, bring your hands into a prayer position in front of your heart center. Breathe into your heart and imagine a column of energy flowing up and down through the center of your body. Continue breathing into your heart center and reinforcing this energy flow in the vertical column of your body. Take your time, and continue breathing and working with the energy until you feel a strong and vibrant energy from the top of your head to the soles of your feet. Notice how your energy shifts.

Once you are experiencing a strong vertical alignment within your body, lower your hands, keeping them in the prayer position, and allow them to turn upside down so that your fingers are pointed toward the ground. Extend your arms down as far as you can. Then bring your hands apart and to your sides, fingers pointing down. Imagine the vertical column of energy in your body now extending down into the ground, all the way to the core of the earth. Breathe into this column of energy, allowing yourself to feel deeply grounded in the earth. Feel the column of energy extending from deep in the earth up through your body and from your body down deep into the core of the earth.

Once this alignment is in place, slowly bring your hands back together in front of you, fingers pointing down, and then slowly raise your hands back up to the prayer position in front of your heart center. Again, notice how your energy shifts. Take your time to fully experience this grounding and alignment of your energy with the earth.

Keeping your hands in the prayer position, slowly raise them above your head. Bring your hands apart, forming a trough for funneling energy from the universe down into your body. Feel the vertical column of energy that is anchored deep in the earth now flowing up through your body and out to the center of the universe. Let your body become a bridge between the universe and the earth, between the unseen world and the seen, between Consciousness and form. Feel the column of energy flowing from the center of the universe down through your body into the core of the earth, and, at the same time, flowing from the core of the earth up through your body and into the center of the universe.

You may experience an energy shift from *being a bridge between* heaven and earth to *becoming one* with both heaven and earth. Notice the alignment of energy through your being as you come into alignment with greater Consciousness and our planet earth at the same time.

Slowly bring your hands back together into the prayer position above your head, and then bring them back down to rest in front of your heart center. What do you experience? What new understanding do you have about the vertical plane? Take your time here.

Recognizing that your heart center is the point of intersection between the vertical and horizontal planes, slowly pull your hands apart and extend your arms out from your sides again, feeling the vertical plane expand wide into the horizontal plane. Allow the energy of the vertical column to support and inform the horizontal plane. Stand for a several moments with your arms and hands outstretched. What is different now in the relationship between your hands and your body compared to the beginning of the exercise? You may notice that your hands now feel more like an extension of your heart. Feel your vertical alignment and the powerful energy of the widened vertical plane as it flows into the horizontal plane. Take time to notice how your energy has shifted again.

Now it is time to move from a two-dimensional sense of these planes of awareness into a three-dimensional experience. While standing in place, with your arms outstretched, vertical supporting the horizontal, slowly begin turning in place, making a 360-degree turn. As you begin turning, slowly raise your arms from their extended position to a position above your head, fingers pointing up. As you raise your arms, feel the horizontal plane extending up through the vertical plane. When your hands reach high above your head, turn your palms out and slowly lower your outstretched arms down to your sides, feeling the horizontal plane extending down through the vertical plane. All the while, continue turning. You may even want to slowly raise and lower your arms several times as you turn, reinforcing the coming together of the vertical and horizontal planes for greatest effect. Feel free to improvise on these movements, playing with all of the positions or steps you have experienced. Create your own dance of the vertical informing and supporting the horizontal, and the horizontal inviting the vertical to be its inspiration and guide.

When the exercise feels complete for you, take time to write in your journal about your experience. Consider then how your greater understanding of the vertical and horizontal orientations of living can inform your transformational work.

Take notice of when your orientation of awareness is from the vertical plane and when it is from the horizontal. You may discover that at times you are floating, not really sitting in either one. At other times, you may find yourself in both at the same time and operating from the intersection of the two. Make no judgment about what is happening. Just observe and see what starts to shift in your awareness over time.

Notice to which plane you naturally gravitate—where you are most comfortable in your daily life, leadership, and service—and take the necessary steps to create balance between the two. Then notice the same thing in those you serve: notice which plane is their primary orientation. As you work together, help them understand the relationship between these two orientations of awareness and find the balance between the two that will most effectively support their visions and dreams.

Inquiry: Vertical and Horizontal Orientation in Your Life and Work

➤ What is your primary orientation on the vertical-horizontal map? Where do you live most of the time?

➤ How does that primary orientation serve you?

➤ What are its limitations?

➤ What is missing for you from the secondary orientation?

➤ What could be different if what is now missing were present?

➤ How could you introduce more of the secondary orientation in order to create greater balance?

➤ How might more balance create a shift in your personal life? In your leadership or service?

➤ How can an understanding of the vertical and horizontal planes of awareness serve us in creating a world that works?

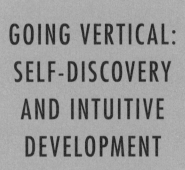

GOING VERTICAL:
SELF-DISCOVERY
AND INTUITIVE
DEVELOPMENT

CHAPTER FIVE

The Power of Stillness

In the attitude of silence the soul finds the path in a clearer light, and what is elusive and deceptive resolves itself into crystal clearness.

—MAHATMA GANDHI

Let's begin this chapter by taking part in a short and very simple breathing exercise.

Exploration: Breathing into the Stillness

Close your eyes and focus your attention on your breath passing in and out through your nostrils. As you focus on your breath, your inner rhythm will most likely slow down and become steady and peaceful. Within a few moments, that calmer inner rhythm will begin to affect your outer rhythm. This may take a little time if you are very tense or stressed, but be patient. Just breathe. Smile as you breathe, and your whole body will relax. That's all there is to the exercise: just close your eyes, breathe, smile, and focus all your attention on your breath. Your body and mind will respond automatically.

Every few hours, take sixty seconds to do this exercise. That's all—just sixty seconds. Keep it simple. Your breath can be your best friend, helping you enter the silence and find your quiet center. It can help you remain calm and focused all day long. You can do this exercise anywhere—on the job, in between appointments, while working out, or while dropping off to sleep. It takes only sixty seconds. Let your breath show you the way to your stillness and quiet.

Researchers tell us that the average person has approximately 60,000 thoughts per day. That's an average of 2,500 thoughts per hour and more than 41 thoughts per minute! Most of the time, they are the same thoughts occurring over and over again, yet because we are so busy in our outside world, we don't notice. However, when we step out of the busyness and allow ourselves to be quiet, we become aware of all that is going on in our minds—the inner chatter that doesn't seem to stop. Becoming aware of the inner chatter can become maddening, causing us to avoid the stillness. Dealing with the outside world, no matter how challenging, can feel less daunting than facing the world inside. Our inner world seems to have a life of its own and can appear to be completely out of control. By focusing on the outside, we can convince ourselves we are "in control."

The outside world is the horizontal plane of awareness, while the inner world is the vertical. Getting quiet opens the door to the vertical. For many people, the vertical is an uncomfortable place. They have little experience here and few, if any, tools or skills for navigating this inner world. Our education and training systems offer many techniques for navigating the horizontal plane, but not for navigating the vertical. The vertical feels unfamiliar and uncontrollable. Our rational minds much prefer the horizontal—action instead of introspection, reflection, and discovery.

The Buddhist practice of mindfulness can serve as a bridge between the horizontal and vertical planes of awareness. Via this bridge, we can move from living only in the state of doing and enter the state of being. In *The Art of Power*, Vietnamese Buddhist teacher Thich Nhat Hanh defines mindfulness as "the energy of attention." He calls it "the capacity in each of us to be present one hundred percent to what is happening within and around us." Mindfulness can help us navigate the vertical.

Practicing mindfulness is very simple. It begins with paying full attention to everything that you do. If you are walking, pay attention to how your foot touches the ground, how your legs and arms swing in rhythm, the flow of energy through your body, the attitude with which you approach walking. If you are opening or closing a door, be fully present to the way you grasp the door handle, the quality of energy with which you push or pull the door open, or the level of care you take in closing it. If you are driving, pay attention to the way in which you accelerate out of a stop, maneuver through traffic, and stay attuned to all that is going on around you. Whether you are picking up a pen, playing a sport or a musical instrument, washing dishes, or folding laundry, being mindful means that 100 percent of your attention is going to the activity of the moment, so that you begin to experience what is happening on multiple levels of awareness. The more we are mindful, the more our awareness of everything within and around us increases.

Transformational Presence comes, in large part, from having an incredible awareness of all that is within us and around us. The greater that awareness, the more easily we access the intuitive mind and the more we are able to live on the Choice and Opportunity levels of engagement. In time, our ability to be fully present during every activity increases our awareness of the impact of our actions, choices, thoughts, and approaches to leadership and service. The mind gets quieter, and our perceptual skills become greatly enhanced.

Take a few minutes for the following Exploration to heighten your awareness of the moment.

Exploration: Becoming Mindful

Begin by sitting quietly once again, and focusing your attention on your breath. Close your eyes, if that is helpful. Put all of your attention on the breath coming into your body and going out of it. Become aware of the rhythm of that flow, of the pauses between the inhalation and the exhalation, and the length of each inhale and exhale. Take your time, letting all of your attention be focused on observing your breath.

Now become aware of your body in the chair. Breathe.

Become aware of your clothes on your skin. Breathe.

Become aware of the air on your skin. Breathe.

Become aware of one part of your body touching another. Breathe.

Become aware of the sounds around you. Notice the many layers of sound—the close-up sounds and the faraway sounds. See how many layers of sound you can hear. And breathe.

Notice what has shifted in your presence to this present moment. If your eyes are closed, open them and slowly look around you, feeling your presence in the room, as well as the presence of everything else in the room. There is no right or wrong experience. Just notice what your experience is and how your awareness is different now than it was before this exercise.

Mindfulness gives us greater mental focus. As a result, we are in command of our thoughts rather than our thoughts commanding us. Mindfulness is a step toward being able to go deeply into the silence within. It is through the silence within that we access our inner wisdom and truth, find resolution for inner conflicts, discover new possibilities and opportunities, and reach a deep sense of inner peace. Through the silence we can drop into the vertical plane and expand our awareness to the far reaches of our inner space. Inner space is indeed our final frontier and the space that must be explored and inhabited for Transformational Presence. Therefore, living mindfully and spending time in the silence are essential parts of the Transformational Presence journey. These are the first steps in expanding our awareness beyond our outer daily world—the horizontal—and dropping into the richness of potential that awaits us in the vertical.

As you get quieter inside, you can enter the space between your thoughts. Those open spaces are the passageways to the inner sanctum of your being, to the heart of wisdom within you. The inner sanctum is a place of stillness and peace. I call it your Point of Stillness. It is a place where you find your soul, your essence, your truth; a place where you can rest; a place where you discover the real, unadorned, unprotected, unassuming you. It is in the Point of Stillness that you establish your cocreative partnership with your soul and with

Consciousness. When you are developing Transformational Presence, entering the silence is one of the most important tools you have, one of the most valuable skills you can acquire. The inner silence, the Point of Stillness, is the gateway to accelerated understanding.

Through the silence, we come to our own wholeness—a state of robust health mentally, emotionally, and spiritually, as well as physically—a sense of completeness within. The verb "to heal" has its roots in the Old English word *hælen*, which means "to make whole." Wholeness comes from solid grounding and alignment in the vertical, which leads to appropriate action in the horizontal. I make a distinction here between healing and curing. To cure is to fix the problem or cause the problematic condition to go away or disappear. Curing happens in the horizontal, but does not imply any transformation in the vertical. Healing, on the other hand, begins with transformation and often evolution of understanding in the vertical, leading to a shift in behavior, action, or practice in the horizontal. It is in the silence that we get in touch with our own wholeness, or perhaps with our *disconnect* from that wholeness. It is in the silence that we can experience our own healing, so that we can support others in their process. As transformers, we must be able to hold a space for healing when that is what is needed for those we serve. Whether those we serve are individuals or organizations, helping them become whole in who they are, and supporting their efforts to live their purpose fully and confidently and to make choices and take actions that support a greater good, can, at times, be a significant part of our work. Transformational Presence means that we have some understanding of and are comfortable with our role as healers in this context.

There are two definitions of healing that I find particularly powerful for Transformational Presence work. The first is from Stephen Levine, author of *A Gradual Awakening* and *Healing into Life and Death*. At an Omega Institute conference in New York City some years ago, Levine defined healing as "entering with intention and awareness that which you have avoided and run away from." Healing is about walking up to our edge, taking a deep breath, and stepping across it into the unknown aspects of our being. Developing Transformational

Presence requires a willingness to enter with intention and awareness anything in our inner being that we might rather avoid and run away from. Depending on the issue, we may or may not need to unpack and analyze it, but it is important to acknowledge the issue and make a conscious and intentional choice about our relationship to it going forward. It's about making the choice and walking the path that will allow us to realize our potential.

The second definition that I find so powerful comes from Ram Dass, a beloved American spiritual teacher. In his book *Still Here*, he talks about healing as letting what is take you closer to God. The "what is" may be something that you cannot change. In Ram Dass's case, he was writing about the effects of a massive stroke and the ways in which his life would never be the same again. We all have those situations or circumstances in our lives that are what they are, regardless of how much we wish they would be different. Making peace with the "what is" and working *with* it, rather than against it, is the healing journey that takes us closer to God.

On the other hand, sometimes the "what is" *can*, in fact, be changed. Making that change may be the hardest thing you've ever done, but if you are really honest with yourself, you realize that the opportunity in your situation is to actually *change* the "what is." And *that process* of change is the healing journey that takes you closer to God. Whether or not the "what is" is something that you can change is yours to discern. Sitting in the silence and entering into deep dialogue with Consciousness can help you with that discernment.

Getting in touch with the deep silence puts us in touch with our souls. For many people, and for our culture as a whole, soul has been put on the back burner for too long. We put so much emphasis on keeping up with life in the horizontal that the real soul yearnings of the vertical are held below the surface. From time to time, we get a glimpse of soul and a sense of "I know I need to get there. I know there is more for me in this life, and if I can just get through _____ (you fill in the blank), I'll take some time for my soul."

When you hear yourself say, "If I can just get through . . . ," then, in truth, you may be making a deal with your soul and not really addressing the deeper issues. If we truly want to develop Transformational Presence, there is no room for deals with the soul. Instead, we must "enter with intention and awareness that which we have avoided and run away from." The shadows lurking inside must be exposed to light. Simply by walking in, turning on the light, "entering with intention and awareness," we can begin to shift things. The process of healing into the wholeness of who we are in our magnificence can begin.

Again, entering with intention and awareness does not have to mean unpacking and analyzing. This is an important distinction between leadership, or service, and therapy. Transformational Presence work takes us straight to Choice and Opportunity: "What do I choose to do with what I am discovering? What is the opportunity going forward? What is the once-and-for-all I am being asked to make?" We must ask these questions of ourselves both as individuals and as a society.

Take time to access your Point of Stillness with this exercise.

Exploration: Point of Stillness

Sit quietly with your eyes closed and your back straight. Put your feet flat on the floor or fold your legs under you. Rest your hands comfortably in your lap. Take a few deep breaths and allow your body to relax, letting your breath find its own natural, steady, relaxed, easy rhythm. Begin paying attention to your breath as it passes through your nostrils. Bring all of your attention to that point of focus—your breath passing through your nostrils.

Perhaps your mind is quiet as you focus on your breath. Yet if you notice chatter going on in your mind, it's okay; just notice it. Step by step, layer by layer, you can drop beneath the chatter. As you inhale, imagine the floor of your current awareness opening. As you exhale, let yourself float gently down to the next deeper, quieter layer. As you inhale again, imagine the floor opening once more; then as you exhale, float gently down to the next, deeper, quieter layer. Continue this process until you come to a place of absolute quiet and stillness. You may have to pass through many layers of mental chatter and distractions before you finally reach this place. It's all right. Don't worry about how long it takes. Just keep breathing and floating down to deeper and quieter layers.

As you float deeper, you may notice that you begin to feel calmer, more centered, and more grounded. You may feel your heart open. You are simply opening to you—your essence, your soul. You may become cognizant of several layers of awareness and consciousness at once. You may begin to understand on a whole new level the meaning of the saying "still waters run deep." You may realize that, although on the surface there is lots of chatter or drama, the deeper you go, the quieter it gets.

As you reach your Point of Stillness, take time to rest there. Rest in your breath. Rest in your soul. Bathe in the deep stillness for as long as you like. And when you are ready, open your eyes.

Notice how you feel after this short exercise. Perhaps you feel more relaxed, centered, or peaceful. Or perhaps this exercise was hard for you because you had so many mental distractions. If that was the case, be gentle with yourself and spend several days with the Breathing into the Stillness Exploration that opened this chapter. Then, perhaps, spend a week practicing mindfulness, using the Becoming Mindful Exploration as a starting point. As mindfulness gets easier, then come back to the Point of Stillness Exploration. Step by step, day by day, finding your inner silence will get easier, and you will start to experience the benefits of this practice. Living mindfully and staying grounded in your Point of Stillness is a lifelong practice. There is no endpoint. The ongoing journey is itself the destination.

If you have been primarily a horizontal person, you may find that when you start to get quiet, you fall asleep or drift away in your awareness. If that's the case, stand up for the exercise for a few days until your body learns to be very still and very awake at the same time. Meditation and introspection or reflective practices are about becoming incredibly awake and aware on deep inner levels and heightening your awareness of the unseen world. Be gentle with yourself, yet at the same time diligent in your practice, and you will find your way into the stillness and richness of the vertical.

An ongoing daily personal practice of mindfulness, reflection, and time in the stillness will provide a foundation for the many intuitive tools and skills presented later in this book. Build your foundation. It will serve you well.

CHAPTER SIX

Soul and Ego: The Fundamental Partnership

I have a great belief in spiritual force, but I think we have to realize that spiritual force alone has to have material force with it so long as we live in a material world. The two together make a strong combination.

—ELEANOR ROOSEVELT, *from her May 17, 1940, newspaper column*

The vertical and horizontal planes of awareness manifest within us as the fundamental aspects of our being: soul and ego. Soul makes its home on the vertical plane, ego on the horizontal. Understanding how they work together is another part of developing Transformational Presence and creating a world that works.

Soul is the portal through which Consciousness enters your life. It is your connection to the spiritual and nonphysical world. It's your essence, the absolute truth of your being. Essence is purity. Essence, like water, is a concentrated, pure substance or energy that, when added to something else, brings that thing to life. Because soul is essence, when you engage anything from its soul, you bring that thing to life. And when you engage in any activity, task, project, or relationship from your soul, you bring life to it.

Your soul lives in both your physical body and in Consciousness at the same time. To use a term from quantum physics, soul is *nonlocal*, which means it exists everywhere in time and space simultaneously.

Therefore, soul is your bridge to Consciousness. It sees and understands the big picture of life. Soul energy is huge and expansive. Its deepest desire is to know and experience its greatest potential. Its natural state is creation and evolution. It thrives on adventure, learning, discovery, and growth.

Ego, on the other hand, manifests through your physical body, your personality, your talents and skills—the aspects of you that are connected to the physical world. It is the part of you that thinks and distinguishes itself from what it thinks about. It is the part of you that experiences and reacts to the outside world and to others. It is also the part of you that organizes things, makes a plan, and gets things done.

Ego's primary responsibility is to ensure your survival. Its job is to be sure that nothing threatens your well-being, to do whatever it perceives as necessary to make sure that all of your physical and emotional needs are well taken care of. Therefore, ego thrives on safety, security, and guarantees.

In spite of its big responsibility for your safety and well-being, ego's awareness is limited to what is available through the five physical senses—what it can see, hear, touch, taste, and smell. It has no awareness of anything beyond this physical realm. Its rational thought process is all ego has to rely on, and if the rational mind can't see something or touch something, it will be very skeptical of the thing's existence. Ego distrusts anything that is not tangible to its physical senses, so it has great difficulty understanding that there is such a thing as soul. Ego can be very uncomfortable with ideas of adventure, growth, and discovery, and it tends to be suspicious of anything that it has not already experienced or does not already know without a doubt to be safe and secure.

Ego gets a lot of criticism for making "bad" choices or being self-serving or arrogant. Yet when you consider that it has the enormous job of protecting you and making sure you are safe, you can understand that ego is just trying to do its job in the best, or perhaps the only, way it knows how. When ego puts up resistance, becomes self-centered, or tries to take over a situation, it may just be doing whatever *it* perceives, from its limited perspective, is necessary to ensure first your survival and then your success in the physical world.

Ego understands how the physical world works. It knows all about the rules and structures of daily life, because all of those rules and structures were designed by egos to create a space in which egos can live together in relative accord. However, ego knows nothing of the vast, unseen, nonphysical realms of Consciousness. In fact, it has a great fear of those realms because to ego, they are completely unknown. Soul, on the other hand, knows nothing of the rules and structures of daily life, yet is totally at home in the vastness of possibility, in the incredibly expansive realm of Consciousness, and with exploring the unknown. Without ego as the physical component of being, soul cannot have a life in the physical realm. And without the expansiveness of soul, ego lacks inspired direction. So soul needs ego in order to have a physical world experience, and ego needs soul for its big-picture view.

Despite the fact that ego has very limited awareness, we give it huge responsibilities and place enormous expectations on its performance. We even expect ego to take care of and nurture soul. However, because the soul has the greater awareness, in truth, it is up to soul to embrace ego. The more soul can nurture ego, support its learning and growth, and give it the reassurance it needs, the more ego can begin trusting soul and its big ideas and desires. The more ego can be assured that growth, transformation, and evolution will lead to even greater well-being, safety, and success, the more it is willing to surrender to the leadership of soul and explore new territory, to step into the unknown.

At least once in your life, you have probably been incredibly excited about a big step you were about to take—perhaps a trip to a new part of the world, a career change, a big investment, a move to a new city or country. Your soul was eagerly anticipating this step and the new possibilities that would be available once the step was taken. Yet just as you were finalizing your plans or were about to take the plunge, a voice inside screamed, "Are you crazy? Do you realize the risks you are taking?" Perhaps that voice went on to say things like, "You're going to lose all your money" or "Your husband will never go along with this" or "People will think you've lost your mind" or any number of arguments ego will make in its desperation to keep you in a space and way of life that it perceives to be safe.

In those moments, if we don't understand both the limited awareness of ego and its deep need for security, as well as the bigger vision of soul, we may, unfortunately, retreat from our great adventure and talk ourselves out of the very thing that the soul was longing for. And as we return to the "safe" life where things are known and predictable, deep inside, we feel as if a part of us has died.

However, there is another way. When ego slams on the brakes, we can pause to consider whether there is any part of what it is saying that is, in fact, true. We can check to see that there is not something we have overlooked or that we haven't considered, and if we recognize that ego has some legitimate concerns, we can take time to address them. However, when we recognize that ego is operating out of fear, or that the risk of *not* embarking on the new life is greater than the risk of losing something of the present, it is soul's job to wrap its arms around ego and say, "Listen, I know you're afraid. It's all right. I understand. We're going someplace you've never been before. But I've seen a bigger picture than you've been able to see, and I am pretty sure we're going to be all right. And I need your help with this. I can't do this alone. You are so important to this venture. I need your great organizational skills for this to happen. So take a deep breath, because we're going to do this anyway." And then we take the plunge. Soon we are in the new place or doing something a different way, and ego realizes that nothing bad happened. It begins to learn to trust soul.

In time, we come to yet another big step. Ego may become afraid again, remembering perhaps that the first leap turned out all right, yet not being at all sure that the next one will be. Once again, soul wraps its arms around ego, asks what it needs, and reassures it, saying, "I've seen a bigger picture, and I really think we're going to be fine. And your skills and abilities are such an important part of this step. I can't do it without you. So take a deep breath, and here we go." In time, once again, ego realizes that nothing bad happened. In fact, it is actually enjoying this new life, and its trust in soul deepens.

A dynamic and powerful partnership is born—soul as the visionary and ego as the strategist. Together, they can bring visions to life and move into action.

Step by step, ego can be transformed from a fear-based consciousness fighting for survival and pushing for success into the hands and feet of your soul. It can become the vehicle through which soul accomplishes its mission. In fact, until ego feels safe enough to trust soul and surrender to its leadership, soul cannot accomplish its mission. It is up to soul to nurture ego and help it expand, grow, and mature. It is up to soul to recognize and acknowledge ego's great skills and abilities, encourage ego's further development, and call forth ego into the service of something bigger. As the ego matures, it blossoms in its magnificence, realizing its full potential as a partner not only in the powerful creation of your life, but also in the delivery of your unique gifts to the world. Ego matures into its greatest potential, and a powerful partnership comes into its own.

This way of thinking about ego may not be what you're accustomed to. However, as we open to our greatest potential, that potential will need our expansive souls, *served by* our powerful and magnificent egos, to become fully realized. It is critical that soul leads the way because soul has the big-picture view. Because soul lives in the big-picture awareness and recognizes itself as a part of a much greater whole, soul leads with clarity and humility. Metaphorically speaking, soul must be the captain of the ship, with ego as its able crew. Soul has the sense of vision and direction, and ego knows how to bring that vision into reality. When ego takes over as captain, we are in trouble. At the least, ego will make decisions and take action based on very limited awareness. At the worst, ego alone becomes overly confident and makes poor choices. We must bring soul and ego together in partnership. We must embrace our soul's vision, insight, and wisdom *and* our ego's ability to harness them for creation and accomplishment in order for us to be most effective as transformative workers and to help those we serve do the same.

Let's pause here to explore soul and ego and how they work together. There are several places in this Exploration where I suggest taking

time to write about what you are experiencing, so you might want to
have a notebook or journal handy before you begin.

Exploration: The Soul and Ego Partnership

Close your eyes and bring your attention to your breath, allowing it
to find its own natural, steady, even rhythm. Don't try to manipulate
your breath in any way; just let it find its own natural flow. Take your
time.

Letting go of any preconceived notion of what your experience should
be, imagine your soul floating out in front of you. How does it show
itself to you? Does it have a shape or a color? A texture? Does it have a
sound? A fragrance or a taste? What does it feel like? How would you
describe it energetically? What are the qualities of your soul?

Ask your soul to tell you its greatest strength. And then ask that
strength how it wants to be expressed at this time in your life.

Ask your soul what makes it unique. What makes it different from
someone else's soul?

Ask your soul what it wants more of from you, and then what it
wants less of.

Then imagine your soul floating into your body. Notice where it
lands. Where does your soul live in your body? How do you experience its presence within you? Take a moment to settle into that feeling and experience.

What is the overall feeling in your body and emotion when you
settle into your soul? Notice the quality of your breath. Is it shallow
or deep, tense or relaxed? How do you experience your energy when
you are settled into your soul?

After a few moments in your soul, pause to record in your journal
any thoughts or feelings you may have.

Now, returning to a place of calm, shift your awareness to your ego
and imagine it floating out in front of you. Meet your ego as if for the
first time. How does it show itself to you? Does it have a shape or a
color? A texture? Does it have a sound? A fragrance or a taste? What
does it feel like? How would you describe it energetically? What are
the qualities of your ego?

Ask your ego to tell you its greatest strength—how it truly serves you the best. And then ask that strength how it wants to be expressed through you now.

Ask your ego if there is anything it still needs in order to feel safe and ready to serve your soul. If there is an issue to be addressed, take time to ask questions and have a conversation with your ego to explore this issue. Be curious, gentle, and compassionate, so that your ego has a safe space in which to express its needs. Do your best to reassure your ego and help it feel safe and secure.

Then imagine your ego floating into your body, and notice where it lands. Where does your ego live in your body? How do you experience its presence within you? Take a moment to settle into that feeling and experience.

When you are settled into your ego, what is the overall physical and emotional sensation in your body? Notice the quality of your breath. Is it shallow or deep, tense or relaxed? How do you experience your energy when you are settled into your ego? Making no judgments, ask yourself how this feeling is different from when you are settled into your soul.

Take a moment once again to capture thoughts and feelings in your journal.

Now shift your awareness away from your ego and breathe into your soul once again. Allow your soul to expand to fill your entire body. Imagine that your body is hollow and that every bit of that hollow space is filled with your soul. Then let your ego expand to fully inhabit and serve your soul, becoming its hands and feet. Notice how your energy shifts. How does this expansion feel? What do you experience?

Now, just for a moment, go back to your experience of soul and ego being separate, each in its own location in your body. First, go just to your soul, separated from ego. Breathe into your soul and ground yourself there—in your soul only. Notice how this grounding feels, how you experience soul alone without ego, without hands and feet.

Then leave your soul for a moment and ground yourself in ego alone. Notice how this grounding feels, how you experience ego alone without soul, without big-picture view.

Finally, return to soul awareness, expand your soul to fill your whole body, and then expand the ego to fully inhabit and serve as the hands and feet of your soul—soul and ego together in partnership. What do you feel? How do you experience this partnership?

Being totally honest, where do you live most of the time? Do you live in ego alone, in soul alone, or in some level of integration? What are you learning from this experience? Take time to record your learning in your journal.

On its own, ego thrives on safety and security. It finds that security in what it knows. It makes choices based on past experience and has a vested interest in keeping you from entering into new and unknown territory. Soul, because it lives in Consciousness, as well as in the body, finds its passion in the realm of potential and possibility. It is always seeking its next opportunity to learn and grow.

Ego can be very clever at tricking you into believing that you have gone far enough. It can easily talk you out of important, once-and-for-all commitments. Soul, on the other hand, will advocate for breakthrough. When we do not go for the breakthrough, we create a separation between ego and soul. When we make the once-and-for-all commitment, on the other hand, we close the gap between them by calling ego to see the bigger picture of soul and to become soul's servant and ally in the quest to achieve our greatest potential.

Our past is a story we know well, and we are conditioned to believe that the past is all we have to guide us. Our potential is a new story that calls out to us, yet ego has no model for tapping into that story and letting it guide us. Ego's nature is to return to what it knows, while soul's nature is to dive headfirst into the future adventure. All information of the past, present, and future exists within Consciousness. In Consciousness, the potential of the future exists just as dynamically as does a memory of the past. (We will explore this idea more fully in chapter 13.) Because of the nonlocal quality of soul in time and space, soul actually has already experienced the potential. Therefore, to soul, there is no unknown. It knows the path to take. However, without this knowledge and information from soul, ego can remain paralyzed in fear, keeping us from moving forward or misdirecting our path. Through the expansive awareness of soul, we can access Consciousness and remember what it is like to live that potential in the future. Soul can then inform ego about the potential so that what was unknown to ego becomes known. Being informed by soul can help ego find the courage to step into its greater role as the hands and feet of soul.

When enough of us choose to follow soul, dive into the potential, and invite the strengths and talents of ego to serve the soul, we begin to create a new and known paradigm for the mass consciousness to grow into. As critical mass occurs, we transform the way our culture lives, works, is governed, and does business. And we take another step toward creating a world that works.

Inquiry: The Soul-Ego Partnership

➤ What does the soul-ego partnership mean for you in your life and work? How can you strengthen this partnership within yourself?

➤ How can understanding the soul-ego partnership empower those you serve, enabling them to step more fully into their greatness and truly walk in the world with Transformational Presence?

CHAPTER SEVEN

Beyond the Soul-Ego, Vertical-Horizontal Duality

> Sometimes people get the mistaken notion that spirituality
> is a separate department of life, the penthouse of existence.
> But, rightly understood, it is a vital awareness that pervades
> all realms of our being.
>
> —BROTHER DAVID STEINDL-RAST
> *cofounder of A Network for Grateful Living*

In conventional Western thought, we consider business, government, education, and society all to be a part of the secular or material world—the horizontal plane—and spirituality, God, meaning, and feeling to be in the realm of the spiritual or sacred, the vertical. We have considered the realm of ego to be secular and the realm of the soul to be sacred. In this conventional model, ego has had no place in the sacred, soul has had no place in the secular, and vertical and horizontal planes have remained separate.

However, ego's banishment from the sacred leaves the sacred with no ability to get things done. Soul's banishment from business, education, politics, government, and society has led to a lack of meaning, compassion, and interpersonal connection in our mainstream culture, and a limited big-picture view. This separation has seriously fractured our social, business, governmental, and educational systems.

In truth, we cannot be without ego *or* soul, the horizontal *or* the vertical. They are integral parts of our being. But as a Western culture, we have operated without *awareness* of their integral partnership and the important and interactive roles each plays in that partnership. We hold them in duality, as if they were opposing forces. When we separate sacred and secular, we, in effect, separate soul and ego. Ego is then left on its own in the secular realm to do the best it can with no awareness of anything beyond the intellectual process and the tangible world—what it can literally see, hear, touch, taste, and smell. It has no access to greater Consciousness. It has no big-picture view. It knows only its current reality and has a hard time imagining that there could be anything else. When we separate ego from soul, horizontal from vertical, we lose our sense of connection to the whole, as well as our gifts of inspiration, intuition, and innovative thinking.

By the same token, in the duality paradigm, soul is left on its own in the sacred realm to do the best it can with no hands and feet. Remember that soul has no understanding of how the physical world works. Because it knows nothing of the rules, structures, expectations, and methods of society, feeling and spirituality can be perceived as being ungrounded and flaky; therefore, they can seem to have no relevance in the secular world. In reality, by keeping ego and soul separate, we deprive both the sacred and secular worlds of the opportunity to reach their greatest potential.

In Consciousness, as well as in the teachings of the ancient wisdom traditions, there is no differentiation between sacred and secular, spiritual and material. Everything simply *is*, with no labels or categories. Everything is energy in vibration, a part of the whole, not belonging to one camp or another. Civilization's ancient languages, all of which predate the religions now commonly associated with them, offer us various words for soul and spirit: *anima, spiritus* (Latin); *psyche, pneuma* (Greek); *ruach, neshama* (Hebrew); and *atman* (Sanskrit). Interestingly, the literal translation of *all* of these words is "breath." The literal meaning has neither a sacred nor secular connotation.

We can, therefore, think of soul as the breath of life. We can define spirituality as the exploration and experience of the breath of life as it moves through us and informs our lives. We could also call spirit or soul life-force or lifeline—our connection to the greater creating and sustaining force of all, which I am calling Consciousness. Whether your belief system calls it *God, Consciousness, Spirit, Greater Intelligence,* or *the Matrix* doesn't matter. We are talking about the same thing. There is no separation—no sacred/secular duality—unless we create it in our minds.

With this understanding, we move into quantum spirituality, quantum religion. *Quantum* means whole. At its root, *religion* literally means "binding back to God." Quantum religion is the experience of binding back to God as Consciousness, of reinforcing our oneness with Consciousness, the creating and sustaining force of all. You could say that quantum religion is all about healing into wholeness, as we spoke about in chapter 5. Transformational Presence comes from living in wholeness. Until we acknowledge that oneness truth and get past the limitations and judgments that come from duality and separation, we remain stuck in former paradigms that hold us in limited potential. We separate ego and soul, horizontal and vertical, and deprive each of them of the power and attributes of the other.

As human beings, we are the bridge between Consciousness and matter, between seen and unseen, between potential and physical reality. We are both spirit and matter; we have a soul that lives simultaneously in the body and in Consciousness, and we have a physical body and ego that live in this linear space-time reality. When we allow ourselves "spiritual experience"—truly taking in the breath of life, living passionately, letting our awareness expand into and become one with greater Consciousness—we feel the most alive, the most plugged in, via our soul, our life-force, to Consciousness. In those moments, we are fully aware of everything around us and everything within us—fully aware of the horizontal and vertical as two planes that together make up the whole. We experience belonging to Consciousness. Suddenly, things become clearer. Great inspiration and remarkable ideas come more frequently. We become living embodiments of vertical-horizontal, soul-ego, sacred-secular dualities coming together as one. This is Transformational Presence.

Although conscious recognition and acknowledgment of these experiences are rare for most people, they are totally available to us every moment when we are grounded first in soul and then in the soul-ego partnership. Remember, soul is the connector. It lives both in you and in Consciousness. It is nonlocal. It is everywhere at once. Your soul is your personal key not only to realizing your greatest personal potential, but also to realizing your greatest leadership potential, project potential, or organizational potential. Ego then provides the vehicle through which you bring that potential into form.

Soul is passion, drive, purpose, and fuel. Soul is life-force. Without soul, there is no connection to Consciousness. There is only an artificial sense of purpose created by ego's efforts and activities.

I have said that soul is essence and that when you add essence to anything, you bring it to life. Adding soul to anything is like adding water to a seed. The seed is whole and complete on its own, but needs water to activate the life potential held inside it. So it is with our lives and projects. The seed of potential for our individual lives is planted within us. The possibilities of how we realize that potential are flowing in Consciousness. In the same way, the seed of potential for a project is planted within that project, and its possibilities for realization are flowing in Consciousness. It is not until soul is engaged that the seeds of potential are watered and brought to the fullness of life. It is not until you engage the soul and align with the vertical plane that you can expand your awareness to perceive and partner with the vast possibilities waiting in Consciousness. Because it is through soul that potential is unleashed, you cannot reach your full potential until you fully engage soul.

If soul is essence, then our companies, projects, and dreams also have souls. Companies, projects, and dreams all begin as seeds of potential. Tapping into the soul of a project unleashes the power of the seed and sets the seed on its life course. By letting the soul of the project guide us, we are guided by its greatest potential, its true purpose and reason for being. Poet Kahlil Gibran wrote in *The Prophet*, "All work is empty save when there is love . . . [W]ork is love made visible" (from chapter 7, "Work"). Your soul is the essence of love within you. Gibran could just as easily have said, "All work is empty save when there is soul . . . [W]ork is soul made visible."

Developing Transformational Presence starts with the soul. Through the soul, you expand your awareness out through Consciousness. Consciousness becomes your playground. And through your soul, you can meet everyone else soul-to-soul. As personal agendas fall away, you are able to be, create, and act from your greatly expanded soul, fully inhabited by your ego, with all of its skills, talents, and strengths. You are in your greatest power and strength, ready to serve the greatest potential.

Transformational Presence calls you to lead and follow at the same time. You lead by your choices, actions, and presence in this physical reality, all the while following your soul and the unfolding potential. Transformational Presence calls forth and empowers greatness in everyone—those you are leading directly and those who lead you, as well as everyone you encounter. Standing in Transformational Presence, leading from soul served by ego, you constantly call forth greatness everywhere you go.

CHAPTER EIGHT

Breaking Down Barriers

When students begin the journey of tracking and awareness, they slowly become more sensitive. Studying the language of birds, for example, helps them open up to the reality that when a fox moves in the forest it causes a response in the sparrow. They realize, "I can actually see the fox through the sparrow."

When they start to read the language of the Earth with the body, mind, and other aspects of perception, then I see them shifting their worldview. They start to see themselves as part of a bigger picture; they redefine the choices they're making based on larger contexts and the impact they might have on others.

—JON YOUNG, *cofounder of the Wilderness Awareness School and the Institute of Nature Awareness*

We are cocreative partners with everything and everyone all the time. On one level, we partner with the people and things around us. On another level, we partner with Consciousness for the creation of everything around us, whether or not we are aware of it. Partnering means two or more people or things are working together as individuals, yet at the same time acting or being as one. Just as in marriage or business partnerships, in cocreative partnerships, all partners are individuals, yet the partnership is, at the same time, a whole. It acts, makes choices, and evolves as a complete entity. It is a single whole made up of various parts. There are times when you can perceive the parts clearly and other times when there is only the one whole.

This chapter offers a series of exercises designed to help you experience yourself both as an individual and, at the same time, as one with all that is—an important prelude to our work with and understanding of how both ancient wisdom teachings and quantum science contribute to Transformational Presence. These exercises will also help you further develop your intuitive mind, stretching your capacity for intuitive thinking. Some of them may seem easy for you, or you'll find you have an affinity for them; others may feel more challenging. That's normal. Just give them all a chance, and you will learn more about how your intuitive mind works. As intuitive thinking becomes a way of life, you will know when and if to use these exercises, or adaptations of them, with those you serve. In addition, they will further open your awareness and understanding of the Four Levels of Engagement and the choices and opportunities present in each moment, as well as taking you to greater heights and depths in the vertical plane.

Exploration: Merging with Consciousness

Begin by going outside into nature. Take a few moments to touch a tree, a bush, a flower, or the grass. Take note of how it feels to touch nature and what you experience in your awareness.

Now step away from whatever you are touching and take a few moments to heighten your senses. Feel the solid ground under your feet and become aware of how it supports you. Feel the warmth of the sun. Feel the breeze wafting against your face. Become aware of the muscles in your body, their strength and flexibility. Become aware of your skeletal structure, the framework for your body. Stretch your awareness to feel your blood flowing throughout your body. Experience your presence here and now, in this space and time, as one with nature.

Now go back to the part of nature that you were touching and connect to it once again. How is your experience different? How is your awareness different?

Now that you have begun to awaken your inner senses, let's talk about context and how it informs our experience. In our conditioned awareness, we can perceive only that for which we have context. This concept was made clear to me on an early summer morning when I was out walking my dog.

At the time, I lived in the southern tier of the Catskill Mountains in New York, on a small, private lake surrounding an island. Quite overgrown and marshy around the edges, the island was inhabited only by wildlife—primarily birds, river otters, turtles, snakes, and insects. Because it was so overgrown, you couldn't see much of the interior of the island. On that particular morning, as I looked toward the island, I saw large black-and-white objects, much larger than any kind of wildlife I had ever seen there. Unable to figure out what they were, I walked around the edge of the lake to get different perspectives on them. Perplexed, I finally went back to the house to get binoculars.

As I searched through the binoculars, I recognized the first patch of black and white I'd found as an ear. And close by the ear was a very large eye, and then a horn, and finally a big nose. I suddenly realized that the black-and-white objects were two cows! I felt both astonished and silly because I certainly know what cows look like, yet because I couldn't see their full bodies and because I had no context for cows on that small island, seeing cows there was not a possibility within my thought process. Cows had never been there before, they didn't belong there, I never expected to see them there, there was no way for them to get there but swimming, and, therefore, I was not immediately able to recognize them as cows. I could see only what I expected to see on the island—birds, trees, and bushes.

This experience illustrates how we see and sense the world from within our own preconceived context. Context creates a setting or background for meaning and understanding. Because we depend on context to help us understand what something means, we usually unconsciously *impose* context on an encounter, thing, or gesture based on our past experience. However, this unconscious imposition of context can also create separation or barriers. A simple example might be how different cultures formally greet one another. In certain Maori ceremonies, the appropriate way of greeting another is to cross your eyes and stick out your tongue. In an American formal ceremony, the appropriate greeting is a handshake. Within the context of the Maori ceremony, a handshake might not be understood, just as crossing your eyes and sticking out your tongue would be misunderstood within the context of an American ceremony. Therefore, the differences in greetings could create a barrier between people of those two cultures.

In exploring new cultures, ideas, or experiences, we must let go of our preconceived context for interpretation in order to break down barriers that separate us from full understanding. We must be willing to let ourselves *be shown* context rather than immediately imposing it—to let go of our preconceived notions of how something should feel, appear, or mean, and what it might have to say to us. We must learn to observe things without first interpreting. We must ask, for example, "What are you? What do you want me to understand, know, or see? How do you experience the world? How do you think, feel, and interact with the world?"

Observing without interpreting, letting go of a preconceived context to allow a new context to show itself, is an important step in developing Transformational Presence. In "The World Is Teaching Me," an article in *Shift*, the journal of the Institute of Noetic Sciences (September–November 2005), Smith College student Laura Carroll expressed this concept very well:

> I truly believe that there is nothing that cannot be understood. But in order to understand new things, I've had to leave behind what I think I know and allow myself to be guided by a different system, where the definitions aren't those that I bring with me from elsewhere but those I find in the places I enter. It takes courage to suspend what you know; it is a risk to experience life and learn directly. But by changing the way I think, I'm changing myself as well, in ways I never would have otherwise dreamed (p. 23).

In order to truly expand beyond intellect and perceive potential and its possible means of expression in their purest forms, we must practice getting out of the way. We must develop the skill of expanding beyond our conditioned contexts, default responses, and personal desires or preferences, and let what wants to happen reveal itself on its own terms.

Therefore, in the following exercises, as much as possible, let go of your context for the things you are asked to observe. When you observe something, step into it in your imagination and *become* it, rather than perceiving it as separate from you. You can always step out again. In the three-dimensional world, you cannot be something and be separate from it at the same time. But what if you stepped beyond that paradigm, entered the oneness of the quantum world of Consciousness, and *became* that which you are observing?

Allow yourself to play in these Explorations and to let your intuitive and sensory awareness come alive in new ways. The exercises may ask you to do things you think you have no idea how to do. It's all right. For the moment, just imagine that you *do* know how to do everything the exercises ask. If you get stuck, ask yourself, "What if I did know how to do this?" or "What might be possible if I could really do this?" Let go of your preconceived notions of what you should feel, think, or experience; what anything should mean; and what anything's purpose might be. Let the exercises stretch your beliefs about what you can do, as well as your awareness of the interconnection and oneness of all of creation. Treat them as games and see what happens.

Exploration: Developing Sensory Awareness #1—Geometric Forms

You will need paper and a pen for this exercise. We begin with the fundamental shapes and elements of nature.

On the paper, draw a square. Notice its two-dimensional, flat quality. In your imagination, become that two-dimensional square. What is your experience of the energy of the square? Notice the physical sensations, as well as any feelings or emotions.

Now expand the square to become a three-dimensional cube. In your imagination, become the cube. How do you experience the energy of the cube? How is it different from the energy of the two-dimensional square?

Now draw a circle. Again, it is two dimensional and flat. In your imagination, become the circle. How do you experience the energy of the circle? Again, notice physical sensations, as well as feelings and emotions. How is your experience of the circle different from that of the square?

Expand the circle into a sphere and become the three-dimensional form. How does the sphere feel different from the cube?

Finally, draw a triangle and become it in your imagination. How do you experience the energy of the triangle? How does it feel different from the energies of the square and the circle? Expand the triangle into a pyramid. How do you experience the energy of the pyramid, and how is it different from that of the cube and the sphere?

Some of the forms may feel very comfortable to you and others not. What is your experience? There is no right or wrong answer; just notice your relationship to these fundamental geometric forms. You will probably experience each of them as having its own unique energetic qualities. Take time to write your impressions in your journal.

The energies of these geometric shapes can be metaphors for the energy within a situation, project, challenge, or goal. Bring to your awareness something you are currently working on. Which of these energies is most present in your situation: that of the square/cube, circle/sphere, or triangle/pyramid? Which energy does your project or situation need more of? What new insight does this awareness bring?

While everyone experiences the energies of these geometric shapes differently, each shape has particular archetypal attributes. The energy of the square and cube offers structure, form, grounding, and stability. Too much of this energy can create rigidity, in-the-box thinking, or a sense of being stuck. Too little can lead to a lack of organization or structure and an inability to bring ideas to fruition.

The energy of the circle and sphere offers flow, flexibility, cooperation, and movement. Too much of this energy can mean a plan never gets formulated and nothing gets accomplished. Too little can mean a lack of energy flow, cooperation, and cocreation.

GEOMETRIC SHAPES

SHAPE	ATTRIBUTE	TOO MUCH LEADS TO	TOO LITTLE LEADS TO
SQUARE, CUBE	Structure, form, grounding, stability	Rigidity, stuckness, in-the-box thinking	Lack of organization or structure, inability to bring ideas to fruition
CIRCLE, SPHERE	Flow, flexibility, cooperation, movement	Plans never get formulated, ideas keep changing to the point that nothing gets accomplished	Lack of energy flow, lack of cooperation and cocreation
TRIANGLE, PYRAMID	Upward movement and flow, sense of ascension, while at the same time being grounded and supported by a broad base; sense of purpose and direction	Projects gain so much momentum that you cannot keep up	Lack of life-force energy, no sense of forward or upward movement, a feeling of not being able to get the project off the ground

The energy of the triangle and pyramid flows upward; it is an energy of progress or ascension that is, at the same time, grounded and supported by a broad base. Triangle energy offers a sense of purpose and direction, as well as momentum. This energy is most effective when there is a clear sense of intent. Too much triangle energy can lead to the project gaining so much momentum that you cannot keep up with it. Too little triangle energy can lead to a lack of life-force energy in the project and no sense of upward or forward movement—a feeling of not being able to get the project off the ground.

Being aware of these basic geometric shapes and the archetypal characteristics of their energies can help you create the proper balance of energies within projects and situations and spark creative and innovative ideas.

Exploration: Developing Sensory Awareness #2—The Four Elements

The ancient wisdom traditions spoke of four primary elements of nature: air, fire, water, and earth. Take a few moments to embody each of these elements. Spend at least a minute or two in each one. Feel the different qualities and energetic essence of each. Notice the physical sensations and the feelings and emotions that come up as you embody each element. Pay attention to which ones you relate to or embody easily and which are more challenging or elusive to you. What do you experience intellectually, physically, and emotionally in each element? Take time to record your impressions in your journal.

Like the geometric shapes, each of the four elements can be a metaphor for the energy within a situation. Consider the same situation you worked with in the first exercise or choose another. Which elemental energies are most present—air, fire, water, or earth? Which elemental energies are missing? Which elemental energy does your project or situation need more of? What new insight does this awareness bring?

Again, while experiences with these four elements vary from person to person, each element's energy has archetypal attributes. Air is associated with intellect, reason, and communication. Too much air can lead to overanalyzing or overintellectualizing the situation. When there is too much air energy present, you can get so lost in talking about the project and everything involved with it that nothing ever gets done. You keep discovering new ideas, but are not able to act on any of them because you are afraid to act before you carefully consider and fully explore every possibility. On the other hand, too little air energy can lead to not thinking things through or talking about them thoroughly enough before taking action. It can mean that a plan is never created or there is not enough communication between all of the players involved.

Fire can be a metaphor for strength, heat, passion, spontaneity, assertiveness, transformation, masculine energy, and volatility. Too much fire energy can lead to impulsive action and manipulated or forced outcomes. When the fire energy is too hot, it can manifest as aggressive behavior and flaring tempers. Where there is not enough fire energy, there tends to be a lack of passion for the project and a lack of action. Even though there may be great ideas, none of them seem to catch fire. Ambivalence and complacence may keep things from happening. No one cares enough.

Water is associated with emotion, intuition, creativity, wisdom, clarity, healing, feminine energy, and a sense of fluidity or flow. When too much water energy is present, you may have an unhealthy emotional attachment to particular outcomes. Or you might rely too much on being in the flow and deny the need for a plan of action. Where there is too much water energy, there can be attachment to particular feelings and emotions, rather than a commitment to action or the hard choices necessary to get the job done. When there is not enough water energy, on the other hand, there can be a lack of personal meaning or emotional connection to the project. Intuition and a sense of flow and organic unfolding may be missing.

Earth represents grounding, stability, structure, order, form, nurturing, and fertility. Too much earth energy can show up as resistance to change and as deeply entrenched attachments to beliefs, behaviors, and practices. Judgmental attitudes can also be a symptom of too much earth energy. When there is not enough earth energy, the project can lack grounding and stability and, therefore, not be sustainable. Seeds of ideas are not planted in fertile soil and are not nurtured to realize their full potential.

Just as with the energy of the geometric shapes, the energy of each element must be balanced within a project for its greatest success. The energies of the elements are present whether or not we are aware of them. Tuning in to these energies can help us understand more clearly why some things are working very well and others are not. It can also show us insight into the optimal balance of energies for the project's success or for the unfolding of the situation's greatest potential.

Exploration: Developing Sensory Awareness #3—Rhythms

This exercise was inspired by and adapted from one in *The Way of Aikido: Life Lessons from an American Sensei* by George Leonard.

In addition to fundamental shapes and elements, life is composed of rhythms. These natural rhythms vary from organism to organism and activity to activity. Our individual energy systems also have natural rhythms.

Take a break from your reading and go for a short walk. As you walk, pay attention to the natural rhythm of your gait. Is it fast or slow, even or irregular, flowing or measured? How would you describe your natural rhythm?

After a short distance and noticing your natural pattern, begin walking in an intentional left-right, one-two, one-two rhythm, counting each footstep. Notice how you experience that rhythm physically, emotionally, and intellectually.

Now lengthen the count of your steps to four: left-right-left-right, one-two-three-four, one-two-three-four. How does this rhythm feel different?

Now shift the count to three: left-right-left, right-left-right, one-two-three, one-two-three. What shifts—physically, emotionally, intellectually?

Finally, walk a short distance while alternating between these three rhythms. Which one feels the most natural to you? There is no right or wrong answer. Which rhythm is the most comfortable will vary from person to person. The point is to increase your sensory awareness of how you move and the general rhythms of your life.

You might also experiment with counts of six, eight, nine, twelve, or

THE FOUR ELEMENTS

ELEMENT	ATTRIBUTES	TOO MUCH LEADS TO	TOO LITTLE LEADS TO
AIR	Intellect, reason, communication	Overanalyzing or overintellectualizing, talking about a project so much that nothing gets done	Lack of creativity and innovation, lack of a plan, not thinking things through enough before taking action, not informing everyone fully about what is going on
FIRE	Strength, heat, passion, spontaneity, assertiveness, transformation, masculine energy, volatility	Manipulated or forced outcomes, volatile or unpredictable situations, aggressiveness, flaring tempers, impulsive and/or unproductive action	Lack of energy and/or passion, ideas can't seem to catch fire, lack of action, ambivalence, complacence
WATER	Emotion, intuition, creativity, wisdom, clarity, healing, feminine energy, a sense of fluidity and flow	Emotional attachments to outcomes, being in the flow with no plan of action, focus on feelings and not results	Lack of personal meaning or emotional connection to the project, overly analytical approach without the benefit of intuition, lack of flow and a sense of organic unfolding
EARTH	Grounding, stability, structure, order, form, fertility	Resistance to change, deeply entrenched behaviors and practices, attachment to things being a certain way	Lack of grounding and stability in the project, lack of sustainability, ideas are not nurtured to maturity and a realized outcome

any multiple of two or three. Then try counts of five, seven, or eleven. Find the rhythms that you feel the most naturally aligned with.

Once again, bring to your awareness a project or situation. Begin walking and notice which rhythm is your default rhythm for this situation. Pay attention again to what you feel physically, emotionally, and intellectually. Then shift to one of the other rhythms and continue walking. After a few moments, shift to yet another rhythm. Look beyond which rhythm is the most comfortable for you and pay attention to new insights, awareness, or ideas that come to you. How can shifting your inner rhythms and the rhythms of a project or situation open new doors of perception and insight?

Exploration: Developing Sensory Awareness #4—Shape Sensing Spaces

Sit comfortably and close your eyes so you won't be distracted. Focus your attention on your breath for a moment or two to settle into a relaxed state.

Begin by perceiving the energy in the room or space you are sitting in. *Feel* the room. Then, in your imagination, actually *become* the room and its energy. Fully embody it. Imagine that there is no separation between you and the space. What is your experience? What is the energetic quality of this space that you have become? How do you describe it?

Now shift your focus and step into the energy of your home. Become it. How do you experience it? Take your time to experience *being* each room—not being *in it*, but actually *being* the room. How does your experience differ from room to room? What kinds of messages or feelings come as you embody each room?

Shift your focus again and, in your imagination, go to your office or the space where you work. *Become* that space. What do you experience when you become your work space?

Shift again and, in your imagination, go to a public space or store that you visit frequently. Become that space. What do you experience?

Finally, in your imagination, go to a space that is very special to you—a place that always makes you feel good. Become that space.

What is it about this space, on an energetic level, that makes it so special? Now consider your project or situation again. Become the situation. What more do you know about it as you embody it? What do you know about what the situation or project wants to be? Remember you *are* the situation—stay in that energy! What wants to happen next with this project or situation?

Take time to record your impressions in your journal.

Exploration: Developing Sensory Awareness #5—Shape Sensing Objects

Look around your space at various objects, animate and inanimate. One by one, become them in your imagination. Experience each object's weight, dimensions, density, shape, and texture. What other details do you experience as the object? When you are that object, what is your relationship to your surroundings? As that object, what important role do you play in this environment? Record your experience in your journal.

Take a moment to come back into your own physical form and ground yourself in your own body once again. Then observe the objects around you. Consider that, as energy in vibration, they are mostly empty space, that they are actually pulsing vibration and that they are in some way having an impact on you and you are having an impact on them. Take one object at a time for this observation. What do you experience? Record your observations in your journal.

Exploration: Developing Sensory Awareness #6—Shape Sensing Your Future Self

Step into a full awareness of your life and where you are right now. Consider these questions one at a time, again moving beyond what you want to feel or perceive to what is really there on a purely energetic level.

➤ How would you describe the energy of this time in your life?
➤ What is wanting to happen next in your life? What potential is waiting to unfold?

Record your impressions in your journal.

Now imagine that standing in front of you is a version of yourself that is fully living that potential. Look right into the eyes of this future you. Who is that person? What are the qualities of their energy? What does that person feel like?

Ask what they would like to say to you.

Ask how they got to where they are.

Then when you are ready, literally trade places with the future you. Fully embody that future self. Turn around to look back at your former self.

How do you feel? Who are you now? What do you want to say to the former you? Then release the former you and claim your new presence.

Record your impressions and experience in your journal. How did you do what you've done in this exercise? On first thought, you may not think you know, but go deeper. What allowed you to perceive and experience energy in this way? How did you do it?

Transformational Presence requires constantly working in relationship with everything—other individuals, your group or team, the room, the furniture and design of the space, the weather, the environment, the economy, the culture, the mass consciousness, the potential waiting to unfold. This form of cocreation involves active engagement and participation with all of life and everything it offers in every moment.

Continue with the following exercise designed to heighten your perceptual skills and deepen your awareness of other people, the environment, and potential.

Exploration: Heightening Sensory Perception

As you begin this exercise, once again let go of preconceived notions of how something should appear or feel or what your experience should be. As best you can, let go of contexts you have for functioning, relationship, and purpose or meaning for anything. Let your mind and perceptual awareness become a blank slate.

As you consider the following items, let them give you context of experience and meaning, purpose, and function. Resist the temptation to interpret or impose your own context on what you experience. You may begin to perceive in a brand-new way. Pause to write in your journal at any point.

Using your shape-sensing skills, become each of these things and let your blank contextual slate allow you to experience them completely on their own terms, each one showing you its context for existence:

➤ a tree
➤ a large boulder
➤ an elephant
➤ an ant

Now bring to your awareness a close friend. Let your blank contextual slate allow you to experience this person as they perceive themselves, not how you might perceive them. Then let your blank contextual slate allow you to experience this person in their greatest potential and magnificence, regardless of how you perceive them or how they perceive themselves. Who are they in their magnificence? How does your perception shift?

Continue this same process with:

➤ someone with whom you have a conflict.
➤ a person that you may see several times a week, but whose name you do not know.
➤ a particular culture of the world.

For the culture, let your blank contextual slate allow you to experience it as it perceives itself. And then experience that culture in its greatest potential and magnificence. How does your perception shift? Choose another culture of the world and do the same thing.

Now stretch your awareness even further into Consciousness. We are way out there now; just allow yourself to play with this idea. What if your awareness could inhabit and *experience* Consciousness? See what happens.

Let yourself experience the yet unknown or unrecognized potential and possibilities for the world. What does it feel like to go to this realm, beyond the boundaries of your current awareness? Again, this perception goes way beyond mainstream thinking, but then cocreating and working within Consciousness are not yet a part of the mainstream. You are experiencing the cutting edge here. What are you perceiving?

Shift your focus again, and let yourself experience the energy of something that existed at one time in our three-dimensional world, but exists no longer, such as a building, a relationship, a person, an extinct animal, a predominant belief, a culture, a government. Where is it now? What form has it taken now that it is no longer a part of this three-dimensional reality? Again, we are really stretching you here. Yet how far can you go?

Finally, let yourself experience the potential of your professional or public life—potential that, until now, you may not have been aware of. What do you discover? What potential lies beyond your imagination?

Take time to record your impressions and experience in your journal.

Everyone and everything is a part of the whole of creation. Being in Transformational Presence means recognizing that everything is energy and that everything is in constant relationship with everything else. When we actively engage with Consciousness, we engage with energy and partner with it to cocreate everything, from the most ordinary to the mind-blowingly extraordinary.

Inquiry: Beyond the Three-Dimensional Realm

➤ What new awareness related to your personal life arises from these exercises? What new awareness arises about your leadership and/or service?

➤ What potential is available to you as you refine your intuitive abilities, reach beyond the three-dimensional realities of separateness, and explore reality as energy in motion?

CHAPTER NINE

The Three Intelligences

Global citizenship depends on the development of thought
and feeling, head and heart.
—ABDUL AZIZ SAID, *professor of International*
Relations, American University

You have probably experienced situations where your conscious
mind clearly recognized what needed to be done, yet for some
reason, you couldn't seem to take those steps. Something held you
back. Your conscious mind may have understood the need very clearly
and rationally, but because your subconscious beliefs were not in harmony with your conscious understanding, you experienced resistance
and inaction. Proceeding with action against the will of subconscious
beliefs is like trying to drive with the emergency brake on. The car
simply will not move. Conscious thoughts and subconscious beliefs
must be in alignment for full success in any venture.

Resistance is usually a red flag in your subconscious mind, signal-
ing an internal conflict. Getting past the resistance requires exploring
your subconscious beliefs to find that red flag and having a dialogue
with the thought or belief at the root of the conflict. Shifts in either
thought or belief will be necessary, or you will need to adjust your
outer goal in order to bring it into alignment with your inner beliefs.

Ancient wisdom teachings spoke of three kinds of intelligence, each
coming from different parts of the body. For our purposes, I am calling
them Thought, Emotion, and Truth. The ancient sages understood
that each offers different insights and perspectives on our situations,

challenges, and opportunities. They recognized these three intelligences as distinctly different, yet interrelated, aspects of our being.

The ancient teachings defined Thought as the analyzing and organizing function of the imagination—the ability to comprehend and process information, to focus, and to create direction. Synonymous with intellect, Thought lives primarily in the head. Through Thought, we can intellectually understand what is going on and create plans.

The ancient sages understood Emotion as our belief about something, our passion for it, and the fuel that drives action. It is the source of power that propels us toward our goals and makes the goals feel real to us. Without Emotion, it is difficult to connect to a project or vision. Emotion lives in the lower body—in the gut.

The sages recognized that the intelligence of the heart goes beyond our personal understanding. Through the heart, we are able to grasp a larger Truth—an intuitive knowing that is greater and more all encompassing than either Thought or Emotion may recognize.

While going straight to the heart and Truth can very often bring immediate and simple clarity about situations and circumstances, most of us rely primarily on either Thought or Emotion. It often doesn't even occur to us that there might be other perspectives or intelligences to explore. If your habit is to rely on Thought, you will tend to go straight to your head to figure things out or analyze situations and come up with a plan. If, on the other hand, your habit is to rely on Emotion, you will tend to be very aware of whatever feelings a situation is bringing up, and you will tend to make choices and decisions based on those feelings.

By working with all three—Thought, Emotion, and Truth—we can gather much more insight and information about what we think, feel, and know than if we use just one intelligence alone. By engaging these three intelligences in dialogue, we can gain greater access to our own inner knowledge and wisdom. The result is usually greater clarity about what is really going on, how we choose to be in relationship to the situation, and how to move forward.

Having easy access to and great facility with all three intelligences is another characteristic of Transformational Presence. As we practice

Thought = What I **think**

Truth = What I **know**

Emotion = What I **feel**

The Three Intelligences

checking in with all three intelligences in any situation or challenge, our conscious awareness expands to include all three simultaneously. We become aware of our Thought, Emotion, and Truth in the situation right away. Furthermore, the more easily we recognize these three intelligences in those we serve, the more we can help them discern whether the three intelligences are in alignment within them or are sending mixed or conflicting messages.

When the three intelligences are sending mixed messages, dialogue between them can help us resolve the inner conflict and eliminate the red flags in the subconscious mind. We can then move ahead with clarity and confidence.

Take time for this exercise, which explores how these three intelligences work within you.

Exploration: Accessing the Three Intelligences

Bring to your awareness a personal or professional issue or situation that is creating confusion or conflict. For the moment, step beyond your current perspective and attitude around it and invite discovery. The purpose of this exercise is to gather new information and understanding. If your new understanding affirms what you already know, that's fine. But open yourself to the possibility of discovering something new.

Focus all of your awareness now on your thoughts—what is happening in your intellect, in your head. What is the story you tell yourself about this situation? Make no judgment about whatever you discover, and do not try to fix or change your thought; just observe.

Now shift your awareness to your emotions. Drop down into your gut and pay attention to what is happening there. What are your emotions around this issue? What is your gut feeling in this situation? Your Emotion intelligence may tell you something similar to what your thoughts say, or it may tell you something very different. Again, do not try to fix or change your emotions. Just pay attention and observe.

Then shift your awareness to what your heart is telling you. What do you know in your heart? What is your Truth about this situation? Again, your heart may be aligned with your Thought and/or

Emotion, or it may not. Each of these intelligences will help you see another part of the picture.

At this point, you may feel that you have gotten the answers or clarity that you need. On the other hand, you may have just stirred things up even more and feel like you are sitting in even greater confusion. That confusion is okay. It just means there is more to discover.

If that's the case, then begin a dialogue between these intelligences to see what else there is to learn. If your Thought tells you that everything is fine, but your Emotion tells you that something is very wrong, get curious with your Emotion. Ask it what it needs you to know. Ask it what it is afraid of. Or if your Thought is putting up resistance, yet your Emotion feels calm and sure, then be curious with your Thought. What's under the surface? What is the deeper story? Perhaps Thought or Emotion say one thing, but your Truth in the heart says another. Be curious. Explore. Go deeper into each of the intelligences until you find a place of inner clarity and understanding. Let the three intelligences help you find the red flag and determine what they want you to know.

The idea is not to manipulate or change your Thought or Emotion, but rather, through discovery, to allow these intelligences to shift into alignment with each other on their own terms. This shift allows for healing, as I spoke of in chapter 5—a natural coming to wholeness within, which clears the pathway for forward movement in your issue or situation.

Exploring these three intelligences further, we also discover that each has a different relationship to time. Emotion tends to be focused in the present—right here, right now. It is a great barometer of what is going on inside of you in the present and whether you are comfortable, excited, afraid, anxious, joyous, concerned, or at peace. Emotion will tell you your gut feeling about a situation in the moment. Be curious with that Emotion, and it will tell you more.

Thought has a broader time awareness, expanding to encompass the past and future. Thought considers your situation within a larger personal context and it may offer an understanding of what led up to this situation and where things are headed.

Truth dwells in a much more expansive sense of eternal time. The heart has an intelligence of its own that is connected to Consciousness. It can lead us to a much broader understanding of our situation and show us how our situation fits within a bigger picture.

The Institute of HeartMath in Boulder Creek, California, has done extensive research on the intelligence of the heart. Its studies have shown that the electromagnetic field of the heart is approximately five thousand times greater than the electromagnetic field of the brain (Doc Childre, Howard Martin, and Donna Beech, *The HeartMath Solution*, p. 33). That means the heart's field of awareness and influence is five thousand times greater than the brain's or intellect's field of awareness and influence. Doc Childre, the founder of the institute, speaks of heart intelligence as "the intelligent flow of awareness and insight that we experience once the mind [Thought] and emotions are brought into balance through a self-initiated process. This form of intelligence is experienced as direct, intuitive knowing that manifests in thoughts and emotions that are beneficial for ourselves and others" (Childre, Martin, and Beech, p. 6).

He goes on to say, "The heart isn't only *open* to new possibilities, it actively scans for them, ever seeking new, intuitive understanding. Ultimately, the head 'knows' but the heart 'understands.' The heart operates in a more refined range of information-processing capability, and it has a strong influence over how our brain functions" (Childre, Martin, and Beech, p. 27).

Until we develop our ability to immediately access heart intelligence and greater Consciousness, going through the steps of exploring the three intelligences—starting with Emotion, then expanding to Thought, and then moving into Truth—can help us expand our awareness step by step. Exploring these intelligences is yet another means of accessing the wisdom and understanding of greater Consciousness.

The following exercise uses the three intelligences in a slightly different way than the first exercise in this chapter, offering yet another path to accessing a greater wisdom for clarity and understanding.

After trying both approaches, you may find that one works better for you than the other, or that both help you in different ways.

Exploration: Using the Three Intelligences to Access Greater Wisdom

Choose another issue or situation to work with, or continue to work with the issue from the previous exercise.

Begin by dropping into your Emotion. What does Emotion tell you about your situation and your relationship to it *in this moment*? What does Emotion tell you about where you are in your life right now? What guidance does Emotion have for you? Take time to explore whatever comes up.

Remaining grounded in the present moment, and in what you know and experience in this moment, expand your awareness to your Thought. In Thought, you have access to the past and future and are able to see your situation or issue from the perspective of where you have been and where you are going. What does Thought tell you about your situation within this larger context of your life? What is its story? What is the greater potential for your situation, as you understand it, from this larger context?

Finally, expand your awareness into your heart. Breathe into your heart. Feel it open and expand beyond your personal context and into a greater intuitive awareness of the world around you and the big-picture view of your situation. What does Truth tell you? What more do you know about your situation from the more universal awareness of your heart?

Take your time here in the heart. Breathe into this awareness and understanding. Breathe into your Truth and let it guide you forward.

Spend time with the three intelligences so that you become more facile in working with them. The more often you tap into them for insight or clarity, the more comfortable you will become with them. The ability to access these three intelligences is a great intuitive tool and another part of the foundation of Transformational Presence.

CHAPTER TEN

Dialogue and Deep Listening

The most basic and powerful way to connect to another person is to listen. Just listen. Perhaps the most important thing we ever give each other is our attention. . . . A loving silence often has far more power to heal and to connect than the most well-intentioned words.

—RACHEL NAOMI REMEN, *clinical professor of Family and Community Medicine at the University of California, San Francisco School of Medicine*

Now that we've explored sensory awareness, further developed our intuitive skills, and learned to work with the three intelligences, we can apply that expanded awareness to dialogue and listening skills. Transformational Presence requires the ability to listen and perceive on many levels of awareness at once—to hear beneath the words; to see many layers of a situation; to sense energies of people, places, and circumstances; and to sense the greater potential that is wanting or ready to emerge.

In leadership and service, we often speak of the need to have a conversation with someone or among a group of people. However, our habitual ways of engaging in conversation can keep us from getting to the real essence of things. The practice of dialogue offers a more effective and, in fact, more efficient way of getting to where we need to go and discovering what really wants to happen. Let's begin by looking at the distinction between the two.

In a typical conversation, individual participants usually have their own agendas, whether that is to get a particular point across or just to be heard. Most people focus primarily on what they are going to say next, how they are going to say it, and making sure their opinions and thoughts are heard. Others disappear in conversations, letting the stronger voices and opinions prevail. Conversation is usually grounded much more in a horizontal awareness than a vertical one. It is usually an exchange of information or ideas between the participants and is usually focused in the past or the future. Rarely is a conversation focused in the present moment.

Most of the conversations we have throughout our day are casual, but when we engage in more serious ones, at least one person often has a specific agenda and a desired outcome in mind. We tend to function as individuals in conversations, rarely recognizing our connection to a larger whole and operating primarily from our predetermined thoughts and opinions.

Whereas conversation is about exchanging ideas and information, dialogue is about exploring meaning and discovering deeper insights and awareness. That is dialogue's only agenda. In order to truly engage in dialogue with another, we must anchor ourselves in the vertical plane of awareness, where we can access the deep listening skills associated with intuition and higher awareness. While we may notice the responses of our Thought and Emotion, we strive to listen from the more expansive Truth awareness of the heart.

Whereas in conversation we summarize and draw conclusions from what is said, the focus in dialogue is the deeper meaning behind the words. Perceiving that meaning leads to discovery and deeper understanding. And this discovery and deeper understanding often lead to new creation—a new idea, a new way of relating or being together, a new practice, or a new way of doing something. Dialogue is not about summary or conclusion.

While conversation often lives in the past or future, dialogue often opens the door not just to the present moment, but also to a sense of the eternal moment—an awareness of past, present, and future all coexisting right here, right now. While conversation consists of individuals bouncing predetermined thoughts and opinions back and forth, dialogue invites participants to come into their full, authentic presence as a part of a greater whole, and to express what is showing up *through* them as the dialogue unfolds.

Dialogue is much more about listening than about speaking. And that listening is done at a deep and profound level; it is listening beneath the words and the gestures to find the source of those words and inviting the source itself to speak more clearly and directly. Dialogue is about getting to essence and letting essence speak, rather than speaking our interpretation of what we might think essence is. There is no analyzing in dialogue; there is only discovery. There is no "figuring it out," but rather unfolding revelation. Dialogue, in its highest form, is Consciousness in full discovery mode.

When participants use good communication skills, conversation can effectively get things done and move things forward. Conversation and open communication keep things moving in the horizontal plane. When our conversation leads to appropriate understanding and action, we make progress toward our goals.

However, leadership and service can reach new levels of effectiveness

CONVERSATION	DIALOGUE
➤ Has an agenda	➤ Is about discovery
➤ Comprises words arising from agendas and prior thoughts	➤ Comprises words and thoughts arising from the essence of the dialogue
➤ Lives in the horizontal plane	➤ Lives in the vertical plane and often gives greater insight into the horizontal
➤ Involves exchanging information and ideas	➤ Explores meaning
➤ Summarizes and leads to conclusions	➤ Finds meaning that leads to understanding
➤ Focuses on the past and/ or future	➤ Lives in the eternal moment
➤ Recognizes the self and predetermined thoughts	➤ Recognizes the presence of each person and what is showing up through them

and power when they include dialogue. There are times when we need to press pause on the conversation and shift the energy and intention to dialogue. This shift allows the communication to move beyond agendas, analyzing, strategizing, and generally figuring things out and into discovery and unfolding. Understanding the distinction between conversation and dialogue and intentionally choosing which one you wish to engage in at any particular moment can help you take big steps forward; break out of old patterns of awareness, understanding, and behavior; and achieve breakthroughs.

The power of dialogue is in the *process* of speaking and listening. The process itself creates meaning. It is easy to get overly focused on summarizing and reaching conclusions, to lose touch with the vertical and function only in the horizontal. When we lose touch with the vertical, we lose touch with the meaning of what we are doing, and the project, relationship, or organization is no longer sustainable. When functioning only in the horizontal, we will not reach the full potential waiting to unfold. We will not be nearly as effective or productive as we could be if we were grounded in the vertical. We cannot be in Transformational Presence. Transformational work is rooted in being, presence, meaning, and expanded awareness and allows those four things to inform action.

Dialogue is about listening and responding to meaning. It recognizes the presence of each person *and* of the ideas that are showing up *through* each person in the moment. Then it rests in the power of those presences and the power of the moment, seeing what unfolds. The ability to step beyond conversation into dialogue and to listen at a deep level is a key to Transformational Presence work.

Several guidelines can help you develop your deep listening abilities. First, while listening, sit quietly and comfortably and look at the speaker. If the dialogue is not happening face-to-face, it is important to still be fully present with the speaker. Remain comfortably still, offering no verbal or physical responses, gestures, or acknowledgment. Just remain open, clear, and receptive. You and the other person can even agree beforehand that while listening, you will be fully present with one another, yet refrain from outward response. Not responding allows the speakers to express themselves and be the voice for what wants to be said, with no worry about reactions, judgment, agreement or disagreement, or interruption. As the listener, take in what the speaker is saying on as many levels as you are able. Listen for the essence behind the words so that you will be able to respond directly to the essence, rather than just to the words.

When the speaker has completed speaking for the moment, you may then respond to what you heard—not reporting the words back or retelling the story, but responding to the essence and the energy behind what was said. Your response is not a summary statement, but a statement of meaning and essence as you understood it. The meaning and essence may take both of you further into discovery as you continue to explore together.

Deep listening is one of the greatest gifts we can give one another. We all yearn to be heard and seen. Listening to one another at such deep levels allows us to truly experience being seen and heard and calls us forth to our full authentic presence. The more we are fully present with one another in our own authentic presence, the more we engage with one another at higher levels of awareness and communication.

Dialogue and deep listening are learned skills. For some of us, these skills come relatively easily, while for others, they may initially require a great deal of mental focus and self-management. However, the more you practice listening deeply and engaging in intentional dialogue with others, the easier it becomes and the more the riches of Consciousness become available to you.

Exploration: Dialogue and Deep Listening

Invite a trusted friend or colleague to join you in this exploration. Decide between you who will be the speaker and who will be the listener. Although there will be times when the listener speaks and the speaker listens, you will keep your initial roles throughout the exercise.

Allow yourselves time and space to settle in and be comfortable, because you are going to be together for about an hour. Take whatever steps are necessary to ensure you will not be interrupted.

The exercise begins with the speaker talking about anything he or she wishes. It can be anything that is on the speaker's mind—perhaps something the speaker is concerned about or desires clarity about, or an experience that the speaker would like to share. The speaker is to speak for ten minutes—by the clock. So that the speaker has no distractions, the listener should keep track of the time and simply say "thank you" when the time is up.

It is important to keep the full ten minutes, even if the speaker feels there is no more to say. There can be a lot to notice in the silence and the energy present in the room. Sometimes the energy is even more palpable when there is silence. So the speaker should feel no obligation to fill up the time with words, but rather say whatever needs to be said and allow natural periods of silence and stillness to be present as well.

While the speaker speaks, the listener is simply to be fully present, with an open and receptive countenance. The listener is not to respond verbally or with physical gesture—no smiles, nods, or acknowledgment in any way. Just be fully present with the speaker. Even without visual or verbal responses, the speaker will feel the full presence of the listener and appreciate it greatly. This may be the first time the speaker has ever been able to speak honestly and openly without being interrupted—the first time he or she truly feels heard. This process can sometimes elicit an emotional response from the speaker. Should that happen, the listener is simply to be present with that emotional response and trust that the speaker can take care of him- or herself. Again, the speaker will appreciate the listener being so fully present and allowing the speaker's full experience.

After saying "thank you" at the end of ten minutes, the listener then has five minutes to respond to the speaker. Again, remember that the listener responds to the essence of what was said and to the energy present, not just reporting back what he or she has heard, trying to advance an agenda, or jumping to conclusions or fixes. The listener should be fully present when responding. The speaker is now to listen in the same way that the listener originally did—with no responses, gestures, or acknowledgment. He or she is just to be fully present and listening on all levels.

At the end of the five minutes (the listener is still keeping track of the time), the listener stops talking, and it is time for the speaker to speak again. The speaker may choose to respond to what the listener said or may continue with what he or she has to say. The speaker will speak for another ten minutes. Again, the speaker is not obliged to fill the time with words. However, the full ten minutes is reserved for the speaker. It is his or her choice whether to fill the time with speech or silence.

At the end of the ten minutes, the listener once again says "thank you" and responds as before for five minutes. At the end of the listener's five minutes, the speaker has five more minutes to complete the dialogue.

Please note that completing the dialogue does not necessarily mean wrapping it up or drawing conclusions or summarizing. Any of that may happen, yet the dialogue may also be left open-ended, becoming an invitation to a second dialogue at another time.

When this round of the dialogue is complete, both the speaker and listener can stand, move around, and shake out the energy of that dialogue. And then when both are ready, they can sit back down, switch roles, and repeat this process.

When both dialogues are complete, the participants should take some time to share with one another what they experienced as both speaker and listener. What was learned? What was easy? What was rewarding? What was challenging? What new insights did they gain about how to be present with another in leadership, service, and life?

Dialogue can go even further when the participants listen to the topic itself and let it speak through them, stepping completely beyond their own voice, feelings, and personal awareness. I call this process enlightened dialogue. Enlightened dialogue is a form of intuitive dialogue between two or more people and a topic or concept. It is a simple process that can bring powerful insights, understandings, revelations, and new perspectives to situations, circumstances, and opportunities. Enlightened dialogue creates a way for the wisdom inherent within the topic, as well as the collective intelligence and Consciousness, to speak.

Invite at least one or two adventurous friends or colleagues to join you for the following Exploration.

Exploration: Enlightened Dialogue

Take a few moments to get quiet and centered. Then invite a topic to be present with you—to float out in front of you or in the middle of the circle as pure energy. Participants will perceive the energy in different ways; some may see colors, shapes, or forms, while others may feel it as a force or a texture, hear it as a sound, or even perceive a fragrance or a taste. Allow time for the participants to share how the topic is showing itself to them.

Then invite all participants to allow the topic to speak through them to the group, opening up an intuitive dialogue between the group and the topic.

For this process to be successful, follow these important guidelines:

➤ Someone assumes the role of steward of the dialogue and ensures that the guidelines of enlightened dialogue are followed.

➤ All participants open themselves to receiving information or guidance intuitively, suspending judgment about anything that is said, what is possible or not, what is viable or not.

➤ Participants do not give advice or directly express opinions. All ideas are expressed as perspectives, as in, "What if _____ were true?"

➤ All participants should recognize that this is a completely intuitive process, that the intuitive mind is the greater mind, and that the rational/intellectual mind is just a small part of the larger intuitive mind.

➤ Participants agree to expand far beyond personal opinion or problem-solving into a higher awareness, where they can tap into the greatest potential of the moment and discover what wants to happen for the greater good of all. It is understood that everyone will be able to expand this way to varying degrees at first, but the more they practice this expansion, the more facile participants become with the process.

➤ Participants do not have to understand what they are about to say; they are simply invited to share what they perceive.

➤ Participants are dialoging with the topic and the greater potential, rather than with each other. There is no cross conversation between participants.

➤ As the topic speaks through participants, participants are encouraged to ask further questions of the topic—not of each other. They are encouraged to be curious and to dig deeper in order to understand how to apply the information in practical terms. Participants should continue tapping into deeper levels to discover what else the topic has to say.

➤ After completing the exercise, participants can talk about what came up during the process. Until then, the dialogue stays between individuals and the topic.

➤ Participants do not need to reach a consensus. Enlightened dialogue is a process for discovering and giving voice to new ideas and perspectives. Previously expressed ideas and perspectives may be challenged or reinforced, but that challenge or reinforcement comes through the topic, not individual opinion.

➤ One of the participants serves as a scribe, writing down every thing the topic says or reveals.

As long as everyone follows the guidelines, no one needs to lead the group to a specific outcome. An outcome will emerge from the process, if that is what wants to happen. Anyone can step into leadership of the dialogue at any time, and leadership can be allowed to flow between the participants.

ANCIENT WISDOM MEETS THE NEW PHYSICS: UNDERSTANDING HOW LIFE WORKS

CHAPTER ELEVEN

The Seven Hermetic Principles

Everyone who is seriously involved in the pursuit of science becomes convinced that a spirit is manifest in the laws of the universe—a spirit vastly superior to man.

—ALBERT EINSTEIN, *physicist*

Having explored concepts of energy and intuition from an experiential perspective, we now explore these topics from the perspectives of ancient wisdom teachings and quantum science. A great convergence is happening now between the teachings of ancient mystery schools, evolutionary consciousness studies, and the principles of quantum physics. Quantum physics shows us the science behind what the ancient priests and sages held to be true. The more we understand and can articulate, simply and clearly, how life works as energy in motion, the more our presence supports transformation in our worlds.

As we embark upon this next level of our work together, I am reminded of Yasuhiko Genku Kimura's words quoted in the introduction to this book, which tell us that thinking, for most people, is information-shuffling. His expanded definition of "to think" was "to create in accord with the kosmic" (Kimura, *Think Kosmically, Act Globally*, p. 6). As you read on, keep expanding beyond your intellect into your intuitive mind. We have spent a great deal of time engaging the intuitive mind thus far, yet as we begin to explore what for some will be complex ideas and concepts, it is easy to close back down to the intellect.

Each time you sit down to read, breathe into your heart and engage your intuitive mind, the mind of your soul. Your soul lives every day in full understanding of these principles. Your soul understands life as energy in motion. So if some of the principles seem difficult to comprehend, pause and breathe into your heart and soul. Dive deep into the vertical. Then continue reading from that awareness. In addition, take time with the Inquiries. They will help you take these ideas and concepts directly into your daily life and work.

Everything in life flows according to universal principles. The mystery schools of ancient Greece and Egypt understood these laws and codified them as the Hermetic Principles. The term *hermetic* comes from the name Hermes Trismegistus, who was a mystical (and, some scholars say, mythical) Egyptian philosopher and teacher. The source of our modern-day understanding of hermetic philosophy is a book called *The Kybalion*, first published in 1908 and said to contain the teachings of Hermes Trismegistus. The mystical beginnings of our modern-day religious traditions and belief systems are rooted in the Hermetic Principles. Each tradition has interpreted them in unique ways to create the foundations of its particular belief system. Yet most people go through life without ever hearing of these principles, much less fully understanding them.

A working knowledge of the Hermetic Principles opens many doors to higher levels of awareness. By studying these principles, we can more fully understand how life works as energy in motion. We can better understand, from an energetic perspective, how we are able to accomplish some things, yet fail in our attempts with others. Then we can begin to more effectively and efficiently manifest our dreams and accomplish the things we feel called to do.

The Hermetic Principles are part of the knowledge base that supports Transformational Presence. You may or may not ever talk about these principles with those you serve, yet your understanding of them and of how life works as energy in motion will inform your leadership and service in both powerful and subtle ways, which will allow you to have greater impact in your world. Some of these principles may seem like common sense, and you will easily grasp them, at least at the surface level. Others may seem more complex. Don't be discouraged if all is not clear at first. We will revisit these principles throughout the rest of the book, and your understanding of how they influence daily life and work will continue to evolve.

The fundamental principle through which all of the Hermetic Principles are understood is that everything is energy. This simply means that the universe and everything in it is composed of energy. And, according to the Principle of Vibration, which I will talk about more in a few pages, that energy is always vibrating or in motion. Therefore, *everything* is energy in motion. This book you hold in your hand is energy in motion, as is the chair you sit in, the house you live in, the ground you walk on, the food you eat, the sky you see, the air you breathe, your body, and even your thoughts, opinions, and actions. Everything, at its fundamental level, is energy in motion.

Another fundamental understanding behind the Hermetic Principles is that energy cannot be created or destroyed. It can only be transformed. This means that all the energy that has ever been and ever will be exists in some form right now. A wooden table was once a tree, and before it was a tree, it was a seed. And before it became a seed, it was part of another tree. The air you breathe was in some other part of the world yesterday and has been recycled since the earth was formed. Your body was created by the fusion of a sperm and an egg, which were themselves the offspring of procreation since there first was life. Your habits are formed out of your thought patterns and your socialization, which have been influenced by thought patterns that have shifted and transformed over the millennia.

This principle that energy cannot be created or destroyed, but can only be transformed, is a key concept in Transformational Presence. It tells you that if you wish to change a behavior pattern, you cannot destroy it; you can only transform it into another behavior. If you wish to change your thought, you cannot destroy the old thought; you can only transform it into a different thought. And if you wish to no longer have a fear or a resistance, you must work with that fear or resistance to transform it into something else.

I. The Principle of Mentalism

> THE ALL is MIND; The Universe is Mental.
>
> —*The Kybalion*

The first of the Hermetic Principles is the Principle of Mentalism: "The ALL is MIND: The Universe is Mental—held in the mind of THE ALL" (*The Kybalion*, p. 65). All is in THE ALL, and THE ALL is in All. This principle states that everything that exists was first a thought before it manifested in this physical dimension. Out of thought comes creation. The Principle of Mentalism tells us that in order to consciously manifest anything, we must be clear in our thought about what it is that we wish to manifest, for whatever is in our thought is, in fact, what we will manifest. This principle helps us understand why the alignment of energy and intention in the vertical plane is so important. If things are out of alignment, then what we create in our lives and leadership will be out of alignment with who we are and with the greater potential trying to unfold.

The ancient wisdom traditions understood what we have come to call God as an energy, an intelligence—that is, the creative and sustaining force of all. The hermeticists refer to this energy as THE ALL, an ubiquitous or omnipresent force in the universe that was present before anything else and was responsible for creation. They understood that this force exists within everything, yet that everything also exists within that force or energy. "All is in THE ALL . . . It is equally true that THE ALL is in ALL" (*The Kybalion*, p. 96). The Principle of Mentalism is the divine paradox: all truths are but half-truths. (Chapter VI of *The Kybalion* speaks at length about the divine paradox.)

Translating this principle into the language of this book, you could say, "Everything exists within Consciousness, and Consciousness exists within everything." Indigenous cultures still have this pantheistic concept of God, or Consciousness, being within everything. Therefore, they see all of creation as sacred. Through our Western religious traditions, however, we have created a separation between ourselves and God, considering God to be an outside force that rules over us in an omnipotent kind of way. The Principle of Mentalism shows us a different perspective—that God, as THE ALL, is a presence within us, and we are within that presence. Everything exists in Consciousness, and Consciousness is present in all.

This is a central idea within most mystical traditions. Although interpreted in various ways from tradition to tradition, the common thread is a desire for knowing and experiencing union or oneness with God, or some great universal principle. At some point in the evolution of Western religions, the interpretation of this principle shifted into a doctrine of separation—a belief that everything was created by God, but that God remains separate from that creation.

Returning to the Principle of Mentalism takes us back to the ancient understanding of all as one. This truth shows itself in every aspect of our lives. Even though your foot may never touch your heart, if your heart is in trouble, your foot will suffer. If you get an infection in one organ of the body, the entire body can soon be affected, because that organ is not able to function fully and support the body. Any aspect of your life that is out of balance soon affects all other aspects of your life. The whole self cannot thrive when any of its aspects are compromised. And so it is in our global community. When one suffers, all suffer on some level. Modern science's Big Bang Theory also adheres to this principle, explaining that all of creation was originally born in an enormous burst of energy. Everything came out of and can be traced back to that initial burst of energy. All of life as we know it on planet earth breathes the same air, exchanges the same molecules, drinks the same water, and exchanges energy in the form of thoughts and/or interaction. Everything and everyone is a part of the whole, and the essence of the whole is within everything and everyone. There is no separation in the larger web of life. There is a fundamental oneness whether or not we choose to recognize it.

Embracing this concept of THE ALL in All, and All in THE ALL opens the heart to unity consciousness. Unity consciousness brings greater compassion, understanding, love, and acceptance of others, of circumstances, of life. Unity consciousness brings greater recognition of similarities with others, rather than emphasis on differences. Living the Principle of Mentalism means seeing everyone and everything as a manifestation of some aspect of Consciousness. Living this principle means stepping beyond labels of separation and meeting one another soul-to-soul, heart-to-heart, as human manifestations of Consciousness. The divinity implied in this principle is not one that separates one from another or makes one better than another, but one that unites us, recognizing that no one is better than another because all are manifestations of an aspect of Consciousness. In this respect, the Principle of Mentalism is the great equalizer. We are all born of the same source, and we all carry that source within us.

The Principle of Mentalism also tells us that there is no place that Consciousness is not present. This includes within each of us. Embracing this concept is critical to being able to step into our authentic power as aspects of Consciousness. Your soul mission or life purpose is the most powerful way that Consciousness lives within you. When you live your life fully, embracing the essence of who you are as a human manifestation of Consciousness and recognizing that Consciousness dwells in you and you in Consciousness, your every act is Consciousness in action and Consciousness being acted upon. Every word is Consciousness speaking and Consciousness being spoken to; every thought is Consciousness thinking and Consciousness being thought of. The first-century Greek philosopher Epictetus, quoted by Wayne Dyer in *Wisdom of the Ages*, said:

You are a distinct portion of the essence of God in yourself. Why, then, are you ignorant of your noble birth? Why do you not consider whence you came? Why do you not remember when you are eating, who you are who eat; and whom you feed: do you not know that it is the divine you feed; the divine you exercise? You carry a God about with you (p. 31).

Here is the Principle of Mentalism: living your life in service to the All, or Consciousness *within*.

In order to more fully experience the Principle of Mentalism, take time for the following Exploration over the next week or so. Keep a record in your journal of your thoughts and beliefs.

Exploration: Every Person as an Aspect of Consciousness

For one week, be keenly aware of your thoughts and what they create in your life. How are your circumstances and experiences results of your thoughts?

In addition, make a conscious practice of seeing the unfolding of an aspect of Consciousness in each person you meet, regardless of the encounter. Let go of your judgments about what is normal or appropriate, and allow each situation to be as it is and offer its particular gift.

At the end of each day, reflect on your experiences and encounters. See what each has to teach you about the Principle of Mentalism and how it plays out in your life. Then consider how understanding this principle relates to creating a world that works.

II: The Principle of Correspondence

As above, so below; as below, so above.

—The Kybalion

The Principle of Correspondence states that anything that exists or happens on one level of reality also exists or has an impact on all levels: "As above, so below; as below, so above."

Imagine driving on a busy highway with five or six lanes traveling in each direction. If a car breaks down in one lane, all of the lanes are affected because the traffic must now move around this block in the road. If there is an accident, the traffic on both sides of the highway slows down or comes to a halt as people strain to see what happened. If a driver changes lanes suddenly or weaves through the traffic at a high speed, other drivers may suddenly swerve or slam on the brakes, creating a domino effect across all lanes. As in one lane, so in another—or as above, so below.

Take time for this Exploration, which will give you a sense of the significant meaning the Principle of Correspondence has in daily life, on all levels of society. It is also a great way to help a group understand the power and importance of the Principle of Correspondence in our world. You might even use it as a topic for enlightened dialogue.

Exploration: The Correspondence Highway

Imagine a highway that has six lanes, all going in the same direction. Each lane represents a different level of society:

PERSONAL

FAMILY

COMMUNITY

REGIONAL

NATIONAL

GLOBAL

According to the Principle of Correspondence, anything that happens in any lane—or in this case, any level of society—will impact all of the other lanes or levels in some way. Consider the following events. In which lane does each event first occur, and how might the event impact each of the other lanes?

➤ an individual taking a new job
➤ a family member having a serious illness
➤ a large factory opening in a community
➤ oil drilling in a remote part of the world
➤ a major earthquake in a highly developed part of the world

> ➤ a shift in a country's national leadership
> ➤ every person in the world having a voice and the freedom to speak

As another example of the Principle of Correspondence, think about your home. Your home exists in the physical plane as a solid structure. When you are in it, it is a part of your immediate, seen reality. However, when you are away from home, it also exists in your mind as a thought or image. On this mental plane, you might perceive your home differently than you do in its physical reality. You might remember a chair or a picture to be in one place, when actually it is in another. Both realities, immediate physical and mental, exist.

The house also exists in your emotional reality, which may offer yet another view. When everything is in harmony within your home, it feels to you like a peaceful place. But when there is discord among family members, your home may feel like a challenging place to be. The emotional reality of the home changes, yet the physical reality, the structure itself, remains the same.

If you have lived in your home for a long time, you have many memories related to it. Each memory represents a different plane of reality, for each memory holds a different perception or view of your home. Some memories will be happy and joyful, while others might be sad or painful. Again, each represents its own level of reality. You may also have a future view of your home as you make plans for improvements or renovations. Or you may have a vision of your home with a new partner or an expanded family. This future perspective is yet another level of reality—one that you are creating in your mind so that it can, in time, manifest in physical form. All of these levels of reality exist concurrently and within one another, yet we have been conditioned to perceive only one level at a time.

A greatly expanded view of "As above, so below; as below, so above," means that whatever exists anywhere in the universe also exists in some form within each one of us. Each one of us represents the universe in microcosm.

In order to have an experience of the Principle of Correspondence in its larger context, take some time for the following Exploration.

Exploration: The Inner Universe

Take a few moments to go to your Point of Stillness. Then imagine yourself high on a mountain, in an open meadow on a crystal clear night. The moon has not yet risen, and there is no other light. You are alone with the brilliant night sky. There are billions of stars; you can even see the Milky Way clearly.

You have come prepared for stargazing, so spread your blanket on the soft but firm ground and gaze out into the star-studded sky. Travel in your imagination out past the Milky Way to the far reaches of the universe and beyond. Explore it fully. You can travel from one part of the universe to another in an instant, just by your thought.

Now imagine that this vast, boundless universe also exists or is mirrored within you. Imagine that your body is hollow, and within that hollow space exists a vast universe of you that is a reflection of the outer universe. Imagine free, open space in every part of your body. If you find resistance in any part of your body, gently breathe into that area and open it to spaciousness and vastness. Take your time and open to a sense of spaciousness in your shoulders, neck, arms, wrists, and hands. Feel the vast openness in your chest and upper back, your abdomen and lower back, your lower torso and pelvic region. Open the space in your legs, knees, ankles, and feet. And finally, open into the spaciousness of your head. Experience the vastness of your mind.

Spend some time in your inner space and experience the freedom that is yours. Then, when you are ready, let the boundaries of your physical body vanish and your inner universe expand into a completely boundary-free realm. You can now begin to experience and *know* that your inner universe, just like the outer universe, contains all that is and all that ever will be.

You are all of creation in microcosm, and so is everyone and everything else. Here is the Principle of Correspondence. Each person accesses different aspects of the inner universe, and which aspects we access is a part of what makes each of us unique. By opening your conscious mind to the awareness of all of creation, you open yourself to the full potential of Self.

As you come back to outer conscious awareness, keep one part of your awareness focused on this expansive feeling, and know that this larger reality is also yours to live within.

We are constantly learning throughout our lives. Some lessons we learn quickly, and then we are finished with them; we don't need to encounter them ever again. Other lessons seem to keep coming around periodically, perhaps in slightly different ways, yet if we pay attention, we realize they are all the same lesson showing up again. These life lessons are meant to be with us for our whole lives. The Principle of Correspondence helps us understand the power of these lessons and the opportunities for growth that they offer us.

Life lessons are related to the soul's journey. In our three-dimensional world, we live in a linear time frame, yet the soul lives in a more circular time structure. Imagine the time line of life as a giant spiral staircase rather than as a straight hallway or path. And imagine that as the spiral staircase lifts higher, the spiral also expands wider. If each life lesson is represented by a point on the spiral, then the higher you climb up the staircase, the longer it takes to come back around to the same point again. And each time you come back around to that particular point, you are on a higher plane of awareness. Therefore, your encounters with your life lessons occur less and less frequently. When they do occur, you are able to approach them from a higher level of awareness.

Because there are many layers to everything, each life lesson also has many layers. Think of a particular recurring lesson in your life as an example. The first time you experienced that lesson, let's say you were at Level I. Imagine that Level I had ten steps through which you had to pass before you could progress to Level II. However, when you reached Level II, you had to start at Step 1 again. When you have climbed the steps of Level II of the giant spiral staircase, you advance to Level III. Yet once again, you start over at Step 1 of Level III in order to begin climbing up to Level IV. Each time, you may feel like you are starting over again with this lesson, yet if you open your awareness, you recognize that you have come to the lesson from a new level of consciousness. On each new level, you will learn about a different aspect of the lesson and, therefore, about yourself. So even though your horizontal self might say, "I've been here before" and experience frustration, your vertical self can say "I've been here before and learned from the experience. This time around I can approach this lesson differently."

The design of graded educational systems, although somewhat different from country to country, also illustrates the multilevel concept of the Principle of Correspondence. In the United States, a child begins elementary school in the first grade and continues through the eighth grade. Then she graduates to high school, where she must begin again as a freshman, grade one of this new level. After four years of high school, she graduates to college. As she enters college, she is once again a freshman, starting at the beginning, but on a whole new level of education. Upon graduating from college, she embarks upon her professional path by taking an entry-level position within her field. She starts over once again. And so it continues throughout her life. With each promotion or advancement in her career, there are new things to learn, which can make it feel as though she is starting over.

The Principle of Correspondence also offers the gift of perspective. In order to observe an object completely, we must look at it from all sides, seeing it from the top, turning it over to see the bottom, feeling its texture, listening to it, perhaps even tasting and smelling it. The same is true with life. Each of us has our own view of life, and even that view will change as we grow and gain life experience. In any situation or circumstance, we can choose to change our perspective at any time. We can choose to walk to another side, to step into another's shoes, or give ourselves some distance for a more objective view. The situation has remained the same, but our perspective of it has changed. As we develop greater awareness, we can shift quickly between many perspectives and see the whole picture at once. The opportunity within the Principle of Correspondence is to develop our awareness so that we can see the many possibilities.

Hand-tied rugs made by the traditional weavers of the Middle East and Asia are another metaphor for the Principle of Correspondence. When you look at a high-quality hand-tied rug, at first you see a beautiful carpet of rich colors and unique design. However, if you choose to go to another level of observation, you will notice that as you stand at one end of the rug, you see the lighter, brighter shades of its colors. From the other end of the rug, you see the darker, warmer shades. These color differences are part of the detailed craftsmanship of the rug. As you spread the rug on the floor, you can choose whether to be greeted by the lighter, brighter shades of the rug as you enter the room, or by the darker, warmer side. The view of the rug and how you perceive its colors may be radically different from one end to the other.

Yet there is still another level of observation. If you walk very slowly around the perimeter of a large hand-tied rug, pausing to observe the rug at each step, you will notice that your perception of the colors and patterns in the rug changes slightly with each step you take. The colors and design, of course, do not change. All of the colors and the complete design are always present in the rug. However, your *perception* of them does change. You must constantly move from one position to another, one perspective to another, in order to *see* all the many shades of color and every detail of the design.

Every possibility of life is present in every moment, yet we must constantly move between layers of awareness and reality in order to recognize and access the possibilities. In order to experience several layers of awareness right now, take some time for the following Exploration.

Exploration: Discovering Many Layers of Reality

Choose a current issue or concern in your life in which you are having difficulty finding clarity or understanding. Then begin the Point of Stillness process that you learned in chapter 5. However, this time, within your first layer of awareness, pause and ask for guidance on your issue or concern. Expect to receive a response, but hold no expectation about what the response will be. Be open to any possibility, and reflect on the guidance you receive.

When you feel complete in that layer, take a breath, imagine the floor of that layer opening, and gently float down to the next deeper, quieter level. Ask for guidance again on the same issue. Again, expect to receive a response, but hold no expectation about what the response will be. You may receive a new perspective or access a higher level of wisdom at this layer. Take time to reflect on the guidance you receive. It's also all right if nothing comes. Just take another breath and float deeper.

Continue this process of floating down to deeper levels and asking for and receiving guidance until you feel complete. You might also choose to float up above the situation or observe it from every side. Let your intuition guide you. As you complete the Exploration, maintain an awareness of each of your layers of guidance and how they were different.

You may want to repeat this exercise over the next few days or weeks in order to continue gaining clarity and understanding about your concern.

"As above, so below; as below, so above." When we fully understand that whatever we can imagine on the mental plane also exists in some form in the physical plane, a whole new world of creation is opened to us. One of the most famous creators of the twentieth century, Walt Disney, claimed, "If you can dream it, you can do it." Whatever you can develop fully within your imagination you can create in physical reality, if you remain focused and are willing to take the necessary steps. Whatever you can understand in the vertical you can begin to live in the horizontal. And whatever success or challenge you experience in the horizontal you can more fully understand in the vertical.

The Principle of Mentalism tells us that creation first begins with a thought. The Principle of Correspondence helps us see that if something exists as a thought, then the possibility that it can exist in the three-dimensional reality is already present. It is through the Principle of Correspondence that we realize that it is possible to manifest anything we can imagine.

Metaphysical sciences such as astrology and numerology can also be explained through the Principle of Correspondence. "As above, so below; as below, so above" means that what is happening in the outer universe is mirrored in some way in our personal lives, and the energy vibrations of our inner thoughts and actions are mirrored in the universe. Similarly, this principle helps us grasp the concepts of seen and unseen worlds. Our inner universe, by its very nature, is unseen. The outer universe, however, contains elements of both the seen and the unseen. Just because we can't see it, feel it, touch it, taste it, or smell it does not mean that it doesn't exist. Just as the part of the iceberg that we see is only its tip, what we can experience with our five outer senses barely scratches the surface of all that exists in the greater sense of reality.

The Principle of Correspondence helps us comprehend the existence of unseen reality. Think about the unseen forces in our lives, such as electricity, radio waves, and microwaves, that 150 years ago would have seemed pure fantasy. Today, not only have we accepted and incorporated the reality of these unseen energies into our daily lives and become more and more dependent on them, but we have also built whole technologies upon them and altered our daily lives accordingly. If we accept these unseen forces as coexisting with our physical reality, why not allow our perspective of reality to include the mystical forces of the universe?

There are an infinite number of planes of reality. We are constantly moving among some of them in our minds. In everyday living, our thoughts vacillate between past, present, and future. The degree to which we have developed our awareness determines the depth and breadth of levels of reality through which we travel. In a narrow view of life, you will only be aware of a narrow spectrum of realities—perhaps the current physical plane, your conscious memory, and your future plans. You will be limited to the seen reality, or what the rational mind can process. However, if you expand your view to also encompass the larger unseen world that lies beyond outer conscious awareness, you open the door to vast new worlds, including the possibility of remembering the distant past and perceiving clear outcomes of the future.

Ego is a part of the seen reality and is most comfortable living in the horizontal plane and rational-mind consciousness. Our culture encourages living by ego perception, which is limited in experience by what the outer senses can grasp and comprehend. Soul, on the other hand, is a part of the unseen reality—that vast, timeless, and boundless dimension so elusive to the rational mind. It is only by stepping into the vertical plane and plumbing the depths of the all-inclusive intuitive mind of soul that we begin to *experience* the unseen reality. It may come at first as a fleeting moment of clarity, understanding, or perception of another possibility. We've all had these "Aha!" moments when we've suddenly experienced a flash of insight. We have broken out of the box of rational thought and experienced, if only for an instant, the powerful presence of the intuitive mind.

Many people speak of having mystical experiences—experiences that were very real and tangible to them in the moment, yet could not be explained by the rational mind. Mystical experiences are actually experiences of traveling in awareness from one level of reality to another. It is important to allow each level of reality to exist by its own rules. We cannot define or explain things from the unseen world by the rules of the seen world. Accepting the unseen world as simply another level of reality that functions interdependently with the seen world is an important part of the journey toward Transformational Presence.

Ideas and thoughts are part of the unseen reality. Therefore, it is in the unseen reality that creation and manifestation begin. The Principle of Mentalism tells us everything that exists in physical form was initially a thought in the unseen world, whether it was a plan for putting a man on the moon or a vision of how you want to redecorate your living room. Creation is a process of taking an idea from the unseen reality into the seen, from the nonphysical realm into the physical realm. Through the Principle of Correspondence, we understand that the idea will progress through various stages of development on its way to physical-plane manifestation. Just because it hasn't yet reached physical form doesn't mean that it isn't real. The more the idea is fed and nurtured in the imagination, the more powerful it becomes. As you share it with others and they support you, the idea

Even though something appears to be a solid object, it is composed of vibrating energy. Modern science has proven that there is constant motion within an atom as electrons circle the nucleus. Since everything is composed of atoms, everything is made up of energy in motion. Solid objects vibrate at slower frequencies, while sound and light, also energy in motion, vibrate at much faster frequencies.

One of the highest and most potent forms of energy is thought. You may have heard it said that thoughts are things. Every thought creates a vibration, which travels out into the universe and begins to take a form. Our thoughts form energy fields that travel from our mind into our world. We are each responsible for monitoring and disciplining our thoughts, because they are creating the world we live in and future generations will be born into. A passing thought will receive little energy, but if the thought develops and we give it attention, it begins to carry power. The more attention we give it, the more it begins to affect or shape our world and our relationship to it.

This idea brings us to the Principle of Attraction, one of the two subsidiary principles to the Principle of Vibration. The Principle of Attraction tells us that like attracts like—that we will draw to ourselves energies similar to our own and similar to whatever we focus our thoughts on. We attract to ourselves the things we think about and give energy to. What you think about, you will bring about. When you think positive thoughts, you attract positive people and circumstances. When you think negative thoughts, you attract negative people and circumstances. Like attracts like. Whatever you seek and expect in life is usually what you will receive. When you set up the expectation in your mind, your mind will respond. The thought-form energy goes out into the universe as a command, in a sense, and the universe responds by bringing the object of your thought to you. We will explore this principle in later chapters on the holographic nature of the universe and the alignment of energy in the vertical plane.

All objects and human beings are surrounded by a field of vibrating energy. We refer to this energy field as an aura. In humans, this energy field is created by the combined vibrational frequencies of our physical bodies, thoughts, beliefs, and perspectives, and the ways in which we process life experiences. Everyone has an energy field. We experience the auras of others all the time, often without realizing it. You have no doubt experienced being inexplicably drawn to some people and felt an urge to move away from others. The same is true of places or situations. They, too, possess energy fields that vibrate to a particular frequency. We are drawn to those places and situations that vibrate at frequencies in harmony with our own, and we want to avoid those places and situations where the frequencies are not in harmony with our own.

Individuals who function on higher levels of conscious awareness, approaching life with clear intention and living in alignment with who they are at their essence, radiate higher-vibrational-frequency energy fields. They attract opportunities and circumstances that support the accomplishment of their goals and manifestation of the life they feel called to live. Those who are less aware and who move through life on automatic pilot radiate lower-vibrational-frequency energy fields. Lower-vibrational frequencies attract drama and confusion, often creating a life of obstacles and challenges. Again, like attracts like; we attract whatever we ourselves project. I am not making a judgment, but simply offering you a fuller understanding of how life works as energy in motion.

The Principle of Change, the second subsidiary principle to the Principle of Vibration, tells us that since everything is energy and energy is in a constant state of motion, everything is constantly changing. Nothing ever stays the same. This reality is very challenging for people with limited awareness. Their security lies in everything staying the same and being predictable. For them, change engenders fear, because it opens the door to the unknown, leading them to stay in bad situations just because those situations feel easier or safer than changing. At least they know what is going to happen, even if it is bad. If things changed, they would enter a world outside of their realm of experience, and that would feel too risky.

For those with highly developed awareness and a broader sense of all that life can offer, riding the waves of change is much less threatening. They recognize that change is a natural part of the flow of life.

They are more secure in themselves and have more trust in the evolutionary process of their lives. To them, change may even be exciting, because there is always a new opportunity, a new challenge, a new gift from life.

Inquiry: The Principle of Vibration

➤ What kinds of people and experiences do I attract in my life? What do these people and experiences tell me about the energy I radiate and how others perceive my personal presence?

➤ What is my relationship to change? How can I become more comfortable with riding the waves of change and working *with* change, rather than fighting against it?

➤ What relevance does the Principle of Vibration have for organizations, businesses, or cultures? How can understanding this principle help us create a world that works?

IV. The Principle of Polarity

> Everything is Dual; everything has poles; everything has its pair of opposites; like and unlike are the same; opposites are identical in nature, but different in degree; extremes meet; all truths are but half-truths; all paradoxes may be reconciled.
>
> —*The Kybalion*

It is, perhaps, easier to grasp the Principle of Polarity by first looking at its subsidiary principle, the Principle of Relativity. The Principle of Relativity states that nothing exists alone—things exist only in relationship to their opposite. Up and down, wrong and right, simple and difficult exist only in relationship to one another. We cannot recognize joy if we have never known sadness, courage if we have never known fear, light if we have never known darkness.

The Kybalion goes on to say "all manifested things have 'two sides'; 'two aspects'; 'two poles'; a 'pair of opposites,' with manifold degrees between the two extremes" (p. 149). Between every pair of opposites is a spectrum, and on that spectrum are an infinite number of points. Nothing is purely black or purely white; there are thousands of shades of gray in between. Darkness is a degree of less light, fear is a degree of less courage, sadness is a degree of less joy. Therefore, the Principle of Polarity shows us that when we have a decision to make, we must not get caught in thinking there are only two possibilities. There are always more options if we look deeply enough or shift our perspective.

Conflict and harmony are two poles of the same thing, and there are many degrees between them. Along the spectrum between conflict and harmony are many degrees of more or less harmony and less or more conflict. The same is true of problem and solution or question and answer; they are two poles of the same thing with many degrees between them. Since they are the same thing, one exists within the other. The possibility for harmony is present within conflict, and the possibility for conflict is present within harmony. Therefore, as the saying goes, the answer lies within the question. The solution lies within the problem, and harmony lies within the conflict. One cannot exist without the other also being present.

This understanding is very important in leadership and service. Rather than looking outside our situation for answers or solutions, we need to further explore the situation or challenge itself. We need to go straight to the Opportunity level of engagement and ask what wants to happen within the situation. If we pay close attention to the signals around us, subtle as they may be, we begin to find the path that takes us to the answer or the resolution.

The opposite of failure is success. The Principle of Polarity also invites us to consider that, ultimately, within every so-called poor choice or failure lies wisdom and the seed of success. We learn to make wise choices through the experience we gain by making poor choices. If the results of a particular choice or action don't serve us, then we've just learned what *not* to do; we've realized another choice that will *not* take us where we want to go. Each of those experiences offers another clue to finding the path that will, in fact, serve us.

When faced with great challenges, the Principle of Polarity offers great hope. If the challenge is present, then so is the greatest

potential that could arise from that challenge—the shift that is trying to happen. When we live in the Choice and Opportunity levels
of engagement, our automatic response to challenge is to look for the
opportunity that is somewhere around us trying to emerge. We recognize that the challenge is present to help us see a new possibility.

Inquiry: The Principle of Polarity

➤ Where in my life or work am I stuck in a situation or a
problem? How can I go deeper into the situation or problem
in order to find the solution that lies within it?

➤ Where do I get caught in thinking there are a limited number
of possibilities? Where do I think in black and white? What
new possibilities emerge when I open my mind and heart to the
reality that there are an infinite number of possibilities?

➤ What is an example in my life of how a setback ultimately led to
success?

V. The Principle of Rhythm

> Everything flows, out and in; everything has its tides; all
> things rise and fall; the pendulum-swing manifests in every-
> thing; the measure of the swing to the right is the measure of
> the swing to the left; rhythm compensates.
>
> —*The Kybalion*

The Principle of Rhythm explains that all of life exists within an
order, a flow, or a pattern. Science expresses this principle as, "For
every action, there is an equal and opposite reaction." A pendulum
illustrates this principle as it moves in a steady rhythm from one pole
to the other. However far it swings in one direction, it will swing that
same distance in the opposite direction. The farther back you are able
to pull the string on a bow, the farther forward the arrow will fly. The
more you allow yourself to experience the fullness of your sadness,
the more profound will be your experience of joy.

Keeping your emotions and life experiences in check can create a false sense of being in control of your life, a false sense of safety or predictability. But somewhere inside you, the emotional pendulum is still swinging wide. When you do not allow yourself to feel and express your feelings, in time, the pendulum will break through your carefully crafted reality and force you to see the larger picture. Your soul seeks freedom and will issue wake-up calls when it is suppressed. The wake-up calls may be subtle at first, such as a challenging conversation or a narrow escape from an accident. If we pay attention and set the pendulum free once again, allowing ourselves full expression, the soul returns to peace. However, when we don't notice the subtle calls, they are more direct the next time around. Perhaps they will come in the form of an illness or the loss of a job—something that demands our attention and calls us to heed our soul's needs and desires. *Soul will find a way to be heard.* Life is much easier when we live in an open dialogue with soul and allow ourselves to feel and experience life fully. When we limit the pendulum swing within our experience, life's possibilities remain limited. The journey toward Transformational Presence includes allowing life to bring us all it has to offer.

The Principle of Vibration states that everything is energy in motion. The Principle of Rhythm carries that concept to its next step, stating that every person, place, and situation has its own energy, pulse, rhythm, and flow. You, therefore, have *your* unique pulse, rhythm, and flow. When you tune in to your own energy system, you discover that you have different rhythms and flows at different levels of your conscious awareness. The outer levels of your awareness will move at a rhythm and pulse similar to that of your outer environment. However, when you go to your Point of Stillness, you find your true soul rhythm and pulse.

This rhythm and pulse of your soul are like your own personal jet stream or wave of energy that, when you remain tuned to it, can propel you through your life. This is your true, fundamental rhythm. When you tune in to your jet stream and ride that wave of energy, you come into alignment and harmony within yourself. The more you are able to remain tuned in to your jet stream, the less you are affected by your outer environment and the more you are true to yourself. Regardless of the energies, rhythms, and pulses of others, you are able to maintain your steady, sure sense of self.

Exploration: Personal Jet Stream

Go to your Point of Stillness, allowing yourself as much time as you need to go down through the many layers of awareness. Once you have reached the Point of Stillness, tune in, almost as you would to a frequency on a radio dial, to your inner pulse and rhythm. It may be very subtle at first, feeling like a heartbeat or a hum. Don't be in a hurry. Just relax into it. If you don't tune in to it right away, don't worry. Each day, when you go to your Point of Stillness, listen and feel. Let go of preconceived notions of how you should experience your jet stream, and let it show itself to you.

When you do experience it, allow yourself time to sit in it, to ride it for a while. Give yourself time to get used to this newly discovered feeling. As you grow accustomed to it, you can bring it back out into your daily activity. Be aware of your personal jet stream and ride it in every moment. Make riding your jet stream simply the way you live your life.

The Principle of Vibration teaches us that everything is always changing. The Principle of Rhythm goes on to say that everything is always either growing and expanding or dying and withering away. Therefore, all parts of your life and work are in a natural ebb and flow, either expanding or fading. There is no such thing as standing absolutely still. There is no such thing as no change.

We see the Principle of Rhythm in nature with the phases of the moon, the flow of the tides, the rising and setting sun, and the cycle of the seasons. Our bodies and emotions also have rhythms and flows. Everything in creation has its own rhythm and pattern. Everything is a part of the order of the universe.

Inquiry: The Principle of Rhythm

➤ How do I experience the Principle of Rhythm in my life? What are the recurring cycles, both physically and emotionally?

➤ How well do I allow the pendulum of emotion and life experience to swing wide and free? What could I shift to free the pendulum swing more, so that I can embrace all that life offers?

➤ What in my life and work is growing and expanding? What is dying and fading away? Is this serving me? In terms of my presence and actions, do my observations here ask for more of the same or something different? Are they related? What must I accept and embrace within myself related to this concept?

➤ How can understanding the Principle of Rhythm help us create a world that works?

VI. The Principle of Cause and Effect

Every Cause has its Effect; every Effect has its Cause; every–thing happens according to Law; Chance is but a name for Law not recognized; there are many planes of causation, but nothing escapes the Law.

—*The Kybalion*

Most of us are already familiar with this principle. The Principle of Cause and Effect states that every cause has a resulting effect, and every effect becomes the cause of another effect. Therefore, as the saying goes, there is nothing new under the sun. Nothing starts a new chain of events. The universe is a perpetual cycle.

We hear this principle expressed in many ways: "What you sow, so shall you reap." "It must be karma." "What goes around, comes around." "As you give, so shall you receive." In developing Transfor-mational Presence, it is important to examine our choices and dis-cern whether or not we are creating the causes that bring the effects we desire. Which of our thoughts are serving us, and which ones are keeping us from realizing our full potential? How do we need to change our thoughts (a cause) to get different effects? And what outside forces do we allow to cause effects in our lives? Embracing the Principle of Cause and Effect means being totally honest with ourselves about our circumstances. It means being honest about which causes lead to effects that serve us and which ones are self-sabotage, keeping us from reaching our goals.

Inquiry: The Principle of Cause and Effect

➤ In what ways have I set up causes that led to desired effects in my life or work?

➤ In what ways have I sabotaged myself and chosen causes that cannot yield the effects I desire?

➤ How do I allow my life and/or leadership to be the effect of outside causes?

➤ How do I need to take back my life and/or leadership so that I am proactively involved in cause and effect, creating a chain of cause, effect, cause, effect that serves me and the realization of my potential?

➤ The Principle of Cause and Effect is active around us all the time. Name some specific examples of how understanding this principle could help us create a world that works.

VII. The Principle of Gender

> Gender is in everything; everything has its Masculine and Feminine Principles; Gender manifests on all planes.
>
> —*The Kybalion*

The last of the Hermetic Principles, the Principle of Gender, states that within everything there is yin and yang, feminine and masculine energies. Both are necessary for full manifestation to occur. It speaks not just of physical masculine and feminine attributes, but of the ways those energies express themselves in life. Strong, assertive action (masculine) must be balanced with reflection, contemplation, and gentle flow (feminine) in any creative process.

The Principle of Gestation, a subsidiary principle of the Principle of Gender, states that everything comes in its own time, that there is a natural gestation period for all things. The Principle of

THE HERMETIC PRINCIPLES

PRINCIPLE	ESSENCE	CONCEPT
THE PRINCIPLE OF MENTALISM	Living Consciousness	The universe is mental. Everything exists within Consciousness, and Consciousness exists within everything.
THE PRINCIPLE OF CORRESPONDENCE	Inner and outer universes	As above, so below; as below, so above.
THE PRINCIPLE OF VIBRATION	Everything is in motion.	Everything in the universe is in a constant state of vibration.
THE PRINCIPLE OF ATTRACTION	Like attracts like.	Vibrations of similar frequencies attract one another.
THE PRINCIPLE OF CHANGE	Change is the constant.	Everything in the universe is constantly changing.
THE PRINCIPLE OF POLARITY	The answer is in the question.	Everything exists on a spectrum, and there are an infinite number of points between opposite ends of the spectrum. Everything exists only in relationship to something else. A problem cannot exist without its solution also being present.
THE PRINCIPLE OF RELATIVITY	Nothing exists alone.	Things exist only in relationship to their opposite.
THE PRINCIPLE OF RHYTHM	All of life has its own rhythm.	All of creation exists within an order, a flow, or a pattern.
THE PRINCIPLE OF CAUSE AND EFFECT	As you sow, so shall you reap.	Every cause has a resulting effect; every effect becomes the cause of another effect.
THE PRINCIPLE OF GENDER	Yin and yang	Within everything exists both masculine and feminine energy.
THE PRINCIPLE OF GESTATION	Everything occurs in its own time.	Everything has its own natural gestation period.

Correspondence tells us that when we imagine something, it immediately exists in some form on all levels of reality. Therefore, if we remain focused on our vision and take the appropriate action steps to bring it into this physical reality, it is only a matter of time before the vision manifests.

With time and a record of successful manifestations, we learn to trust that if we align the energies properly, things will indeed happen in their own time. With trust, we are able to let go of the sense of urgency when manifesting a vision. Hurry is a symptom of fear that we will not accomplish our goal. In response to that fear, we try to speed things along to ensure that manifestation will occur. But when we live the Principle of Mentalism and know that we are held in greater Consciousness and that Consciousness is in us, we trust more easily in an evolutionary intelligence to guide the way. When we are in proper alignment in the vertical plane, maintain a balance of masculine and feminine energies, *and* allow for the necessary gestation period, manifestation will occur.

Inquiry: The Principle of Gender

➤ How well do I balance strong, assertive action with reflection, contemplation, and gentle flow?

➤ Do I trust that my visions will manifest, or do I try to manipulate results quickly out of fear that they may never happen? If I do not trust that they will happen, how can I shift my attitude and grow into faith?

➤ Name some specific ways in which an understanding of the Principle of Gender could serve organizations, businesses, and governments.

The seven Hermetic Principles are solid building blocks for Transformational Presence work and for creating a world that works. When we partner with these principles, we create a synergy that can bring extraordinary results. Our task is to become masters at understanding and applying them.

CHAPTER TWELVE

The View from the Field

I discovered the new way of doing science when I discovered
spirit. Spirit was the natural basis of my being. The material
world of quantum physics is just possibility. It is through the
conversion of possibility into actuality, that consciousness
creates the manifest world. . . . The universe is self-aware, but
it is self-aware through us. . . . [N]ow that I recognized that
consciousness was the ground of being, within months all the
problems of quantum measurement theory, the measurement
paradoxes, just melted away.

—Amit Goswami, *physicist and author of*
The Self-Aware Universe

Ancient wisdom traditions taught that if you want to understand
the universe, you must first understand yourself. Visionary scientist and inventor Buckminster Fuller said, on the other hand, that
if we want to understand the human condition, we must first understand the universe. Transformational Presence work recognizes the
deep soul wisdom within us *as a part of* the greater wisdom available through the all-pervasive vibrational field of energy known as
the quantum field. In Transformational Presence development, we
explore the inner world to understand the outer world, and we explore
the outer world to more fully understand our inner realms. The Principle of Correspondence, "As above, so below; as below, so above,"
helps us understand that each tells us something about the other and
how each impacts the ongoing creation of the other.

We continue our journey by peering into the realm of quantum physics to understand some basic concepts of this fundamental reality. Not being a scientist, I've done my best to translate big concepts into simple and understandable language. This chapter is not intended to be a scientific study, but a very basic, layperson's guide to this complex and fascinating foundation of reality, so that we may apply these principles to leadership and service. At times, things may seem a bit technical, but stay with me. We are laying another important part of the foundation for Transformational Presence.

Classical Physics

Physics is the study of matter, energy, space, and time, and how they relate to one another. *Classical physics* refers to this science as it was understood prior to the establishment of quantum physics in the early twentieth century. We begin by reviewing some of classical physics' basic laws and assumptions that explain how our physical, three-dimensional, "real" world works. This review may seem elementary, yet it helps us understand how these laws and assumptions have been challenged by or simply do not exist in quantum theory.

First, classical physics assumes that the physical world as we perceive it through our five outer senses is real and that things exist whether or not we, or any other conscious being, are present to interact with them. In other words, a chair in your living room is real as you see it, touch it, and feel it, and it exists whether or not you are at home to look at it or sit in it. Classical physics also assumes that space is fixed, absolute, and measurable, and that time within that space is linear. This means that the chair occupies a precise space within your living room, and it has specific dimensions that can be measured. The chair was in that spot yesterday and last week, and it will be there tomorrow and next week unless someone or some outside force moves it.

Second, the laws of classical physics state that objects or events must come into direct contact with one another in order to effect or influence one another. If objects or events are not in direct contact with one another, neither can have any impact on the other. In other words, the sofa in your living room has absolutely no impact on the chair unless the sofa is pushed against the chair and, as a result, moves the chair. Even if the sofa is pushed against the chair, the movement of the sofa and chair has no impact on the location or condition of the bed in your bedroom. The pieces of furniture in different rooms have no relationship to one another. In physics, this concept is known as *locality*. Anything that happens is local to that physical space and time and happens only in that space and time—nowhere else. Furthermore, classical physics tells us that the chair is in one specific location and, therefore, not in another specific location. It can only be in one place at a time.

Third, a cause-and-effect sequence can happen only in a linear time frame, and time can move only forward. There is no other possibility. Time cannot move backward, nor can we rearrange time so that a sequence of events is altered. When the sofa pushes against the chair and the chair moves, thereby dragging the rug with it, this movement has now happened in that particular sequence. We cannot go back in time and instead push the chair against the sofa, or rearrange the sequence so that it begins with pulling the rug. Furthermore, this cause-and-effect movement of the chair, sofa, and rug is not retroactive; just because the furniture was moved today does not mean that it was in its new arrangement yesterday. Yesterday, the chair, sofa, and rug were all in their former arrangements. However, unless they are moved again, they will be in this new arrangement tomorrow.

Finally, classical physics tells us that everything in nature flows in a continuous, space-time dimension; there are no jumps in space and time. This means that there are no realities other than this three-dimensional space and linear time. Therefore, it is not possible for time or space to be anything other than how we currently measure them in our material world. The chair cannot dematerialize from its current spot in your living room and instantly rematerialize in the bedroom. Nor can the chair be in one time frame now and in a moment move to next week or last year. In the realm of classical physics, there is only one dimension of time: this linear time sequence of minutes passing into hours into days. Today cannot instantly become next week or last year. This moment in time can only be this moment in time.

As a Western culture, we live our daily lives from these assumptions, and, for the most part, they work well for us—that is, as long as we want to function on only one plane of existence, a plane where we can physically see, touch, feel, and experience things only with our five outer senses. However, if we consider that perhaps there are other realities or possibilities happening beyond the seen world, we have to look beyond these classical assumptions. The discoveries of quantum physics show us a whole other world hidden beneath the surface of our three-dimensional reality—a world that includes a radically expanded potential for how we live and create. And, if we become facile with this world, it can offer a very different and exciting new paradigm for leadership and service.

Quantum physicists are quick to point out that the laws of classical physics are not discarded once you enter the realm of quantum physics. However, these laws apply only to the physical, three-dimensional reality. While classical physics would argue that there is only one reality or dimension of existence, quantum physics shows us that there are many realities and those realities operate by different sets of rules.

This idea is particularly important as we consider new paradigms of leadership and service. Solution-based practices, project development and management, and goal accomplishment are mostly based on the paradigms of classical physics and work primarily with the three-dimensional, physical reality. Their starting place is the current reality. Transformational leadership and service, on the other hand, work with multiple dimensions and realities. Their starting place is potential. Solution-based or transactional practices rely primarily on the rational, intellectual mind, which operates in a classical-physics paradigm, while transformational work relies on the greater intuitive mind, which has the ability to encompass the more expansive quantum-physics paradigm.

Quantum Physics

The early explorers of the quantum realm discovered that each time they asked a question of this new realm, the answer was a paradox, and the more they strove for clarity, the stronger the paradoxes became.

They finally had to accept that paradox is a part of the intrinsic nature of quantum physics. Paradox is normal; it appears abnormal only when viewed through the lens of classical physics. For example, classical physics believes that all things are separate and have no relationship to one another unless they come into physical contact. Within this classical context, the statement "I am an individual separate and distinct from the universe, *and* the universe and I are one" would be a paradox that could not be explained. However, within the context of quantum theory, this statement makes perfect sense. To the hermeticists, this statement encompasses the Principles of Mentalism and Polarity.

While sitting in a three-dimensional, either-or reality and engaging with the concepts of this book through your rational-intellectual mind, the quantum world may seem paradoxical and not understandable. However, when you slide into a multidimensional, "both-and" reality through your intuitive mind, the quantum begins to make sense.

One of the most powerful tools for sliding into a multidimensional realm is the question "What if?" When something is really hard to understand, simply asking "What if this were possible?" can often help you move into a place where you can at least consider other ideas and play with them. Allowing yourself to play with ideas keeps you from getting bogged down in rational analyzation. Your intuitive mind already lives in this quantum world of Consciousness. Remember, the intuitive mind is the mind of the soul, and the soul lives both in your physical body and out in Consciousness at the same time. Asking "What if?" can open the door to your intuitive intelligence. Asking "What if?" takes you from horizontal awareness into the vertical.

Let's look at these laws and assumptions of classical physics and see what those early quantum explorers discovered. They first realized that things are not fixed and solid, but made up of constantly vibrating, moving, and changing packets of light called quanta. In fact, those vibrating packets of light are a part of an enormous, undulating, pulsing sea of energy now known as the quantum field—a field of energy that surrounds us, is within us, connects us with all of creation, and has intelligence. Edgar Mitchell, former astronaut, moon explorer, and founder of the Institute of Noetic Sciences, describes it as "an intelligent, self-organizing, creative, learning, trial and error, evolving, participatory, interactive, evolutionary, nonlocally connected system" (Institute of Noetic Sciences' *Shift in Action* member audio program, 2007, track 28). Lynne McTaggart, author of *The Field: The Quest for the Secret Force of the Universe*, writes, "Human beings and all living things are a coalescence of energy connected to every other thing in the world. This pulsating energy field is the central engine of our being and our consciousness, the alpha and omega of our existence" (pp. xiii–xiv).

A field is an invisible energetic space created by the person, situation, condition, or idea at the center of that space. British biologist Rupert Sheldrake defined fields as "nonmaterial regions of influence—invisible forces that structure space or behavior" (Jaworski, *Synchronicity*, p. 149). The earth's gravitational field is one example: we can't see it, but it is, nevertheless, real, and we all accept it as real.

The quantum field is everywhere. Quantum mechanics, the study of the behavior of the quantum field, tells us that at the quantum level, everything is made up of mostly empty space, *and* that empty space is teeming with activity. The quantum field is a dynamic web of inseparable energy patterns encompassing the whole universe. Through this web, everything is connected to everything else.

You might ask, why aren't we aware of this quantum field in daily interactions with our environment? In simple terms, we deal with matter in its gross form—billions of particles joined together to form what we perceive as solid objects. However, if we were to examine those objects at the particle level, we would see there is an entirely different reality hidden inside what we consider to be the real world. That hidden world is composed of quanta vibrating at different frequencies. When these light packets vibrate very slowly, they might join together to form rocks or minerals. When they vibrate at a somewhat higher frequency, they might take form as plants, animals, or people. When they vibrate so fast that we are no longer able to see them, these light packets could take the form of radio or television waves. However, they all still consist of vibrating light.

In our three-dimensional reality, we observe a ball flying through the air. If we could see into the quantum reality, we would observe a series of quanta, or bursts of light, moving in rapid succession, similar to the way still frames move in quick succession to create a movie. When we watch a movie, our eyes see the individual frames, but our brain averages them all together to perceive an illusion of movement. So it is with the ball flying through the air. In the three-dimensional reality, the mind averages together the series of quanta to create our perception that the ball is flying through the air. Therefore, when we observe a ball flying through the air, you could say that we are observing two realities at the same time. In the physical, three-dimensional reality we see a solid object—a ball—flying through space and time. The ball appears to be constantly changing location, and there is a span of time from when the ball began its flight until it falls to the ground. Yet in the quantum reality, there is only a series of bursts of light.

The classical physics concept of locality is contrasted in quantum physics by nonlocality. At the quantum level, particles are not fixed in a specific location in space and time; everything exists as vibrating information. This vibrating information is nonlocal, which means that it exists everywhere throughout time and space simultaneously.

Nonlocality also tells us objects that appear separate are actually connected by a web of energy that is everywhere at the same time. This means that things *do not* need to have physical contact in order to have an impact on one another. Quantum particles can influence one another instantaneously, regardless of their proximity, with no physical exchange of energy or force. It seems that once quantum particles have come into contact with one another, they remain connected energetically even when separated physically, so that the action of one immediately influences the state of the other. Imagine two particles that have been together as a pair, forming a two-particle system. Each particle spins in a particular direction. If you separate the particles, take one to Paris and one to San Francisco, and then change the direction of the spin of the particle in Paris, the particle in San Francisco will simultaneously change its spin direction. In quantum physics, this principle is known as Bell's Theorem, and it proves that all matter is separate and connected at the same time (Jaworski, *Synchronicity*, p. 79). Communication between objects in the quantum field happens instantaneously and automatically. Deepak Chopra invites us to take our understanding of this a step further, beyond communication and into communion. Communication, he explains, implies an energy or information *exchange* between separate entities. However, in a nonlocal environment, there is no separation and no energy or information exchange. Everything, everywhere, is in communion within the oneness (Institute of Noetic Sciences, *Shift in Action* member audio program, 2007). Communion helps explain how you intuitively know who is calling when the phone rings, or how a mother senses something has happened to her child at the precise moment that it happened, even though the child is now an adult and lives thousands of miles away. We will explore the relationship of these principles to intuition and mystical experience more fully in the next chapter.

Waves and Particles

Matter, at its most fundamental level, is made up of vibrating packets of energy. These packets of energy sometimes behave like particles, taking on a specific form and occupying a specific time and space. At other times, they behave like waves of energy, vibrating over a larger space and time and taking no specific form. The idea that packets of energy can behave like both waves and particles at the same time is known as wave-particle theory. In wave form, these quantum packets are nonlocal. Until they collapse into particles, they do not have a specific time-space location; they are everywhere at the same time. These waves are actually pure potential—energy that has not yet taken on a specific shape or form, but is capable of taking any form. Once they collapse into particles, they have time-space location. The quantum field is made up of constant and continuous interactions between particles.

WAVE = pure potential without specific form, time, and location

PARTICLE = three-dimensional reality in specific form, time, and location

---

Physicist Werner Heisenberg gave us another key to understanding this wave-particle concept. His Heisenberg Uncertainty Principle states that you cannot know the location of a particle and, at the same time, know how fast it is traveling or spinning. When you plot a specific location of a particle, in that moment, there is no movement. Since it is standing still, you cannot measure its speed. On the other hand, if you are measuring its speed, then the particle is in motion and, therefore, you cannot pinpoint a specific location. You can only observe and predict its trajectory.

The Heisenberg Uncertainty Principle can help us understand how we view process in projects. When the energy is high and things are happening quickly, you cannot pinpoint exactly where things are at any one moment. You might say that they are "in flux," "in transition," or "coming together," but you can't state precisely where things are. Things might even feel somewhat chaotic or out of control—in a flow and having a life of their own. What you do have a sense of is how fast or slow things are moving, as well as what is starting to unfold. What you sense is the project in wave form. You're perceiving the *potential* of the project as the potential begins to take form.

On the other hand, when you know exactly where things are at every moment of a project and are in complete control of the creative process, chances are things are not in a flow, flux, or transition. They are standing still. Essentially, they have collapsed into particle form. The project and its outcomes have a specific place in time and space.

The Heisenberg Uncertainty Principle tells us that if we really want to see movement, creativity, change, and transformation, we have to be willing to not know precisely where things are all the time. We have to surrender to the movement. In other words, we must stay plugged in to potential.

Inquiry: The Heisenberg Uncertainty Principle

Bring to mind a project in which you're currently involved. Would you say it is in wave or particle form? Are you allowing it to be in creative flow and flux, or are you holding on tightly to control the process? Or is it in so much flow that nothing is coming into form? Is it time to move the project from a place of potential (wave) to a more concrete place (particle), or is it, perhaps, time to return to the original potential of the project in order to reinvigorate it and those involved?

The Participant-Observer

So what causes the energy packets to change from wave into particle? This takes us to a concept known in quantum physics as the participant-observer. In McTaggart's words, "an event in the subatomic world exists in all possible states until the act of observing or measuring it 'freezes' it, or pins it down to a single state. This process is known as the collapse of the wave function, where 'wave function' means the state of all possibilities" (*The Field*, p. 103).

For example, let's say you are going to build a house. In the wave of potential, there are an infinite number of possible designs you could choose for your new house. Until you make a choice, any of the infinite number of designs are possibilities. However, at the moment that you make a choice and start to build, the wave collapses into particle; a specific form that was just one of the many possibilities is now taking shape.

When we participate in or observe anything in its wave form, it collapses into particle form. According to quantum theory, when we are not participating in or observing a particular aspect, it returns to wave form—pure potential. There is no space (location) or time information available. The wave state is the immeasurable potential for all that was, is, and will ever be. In the wave state, there are no individual or separate objects, thoughts, or people. There is only pure vibrating energy that has the potential to collapse into any particle form. How we choose to engage the wave and give shape to the potential determines the form that will be created.

Chapter 8 spoke of oneness and differentiation. The corollary in quantum theory is wave and particle. Once a wave collapses into a particle, the particle is now a differentiation of the oneness energy that made up the wave. The wave state represents the oneness of all—everything is made up of the same energy. The particle state represents the differentiation of the oneness—the energy takes different specific forms. Thus, the oneness and the differentiation, the unity and the individuality, exist at the same time.

A key difference between the laws of classical and quantum physics is the role of the observer within "reality." In classical physics, the observer is the one performing the experiment or engaged with the phenomenon in the moment. That observer is considered a completely separate and uninvolved entity, observing a universe that, according to its principles, exists and evolves whether or not the observer is present.

Quantum physics, on the other hand, recognizes the universe as a sea of vibrating energy, and because everything is in constant vibration, it exists as potential, rather than as a set reality. Quantum theorists discovered, however, that as soon as a wave of potential is observed or measured in some way, it collapses into a fixed form. Therefore, they began using the term *participant-observer*, rather than just *observer*. *Observer* implies that the person has no influence on what he or she is observing. However, because it is the observer who, in fact, influences what form the potential will take, he or she becomes a participant in creation, in addition to being an observer. There is a relationship between participant-observer and what is being observed. *It is the act of observing that causes the wave to collapse into a particle, that causes the potential to take form.* Until the sea of potential is observed, it has no set physical form. Until potential has a three-dimensional partner—a participant-observer—it cannot manifest in physical form.

This discovery shattered former beliefs about the nature of reality. It became clear that the *conscious awareness* of the participant-observer is what brings the observed into being. Nothing exists at the quantum level as an actual thing unless we have some relationship to it or perception of it. This means that at the quantum level—the building-blocks level—we are creating our world minute by minute, hour by hour, day by day. In fact, quantum physicists tell us that our universe is being re-created tens of thousands of times every second.

The participant-observer principle is very important for transformational work. Waves collapsing into particles can be compared to potential turning into results, or idea moving into action. As we perceive the potential available to us, *we must realize that the potential needs us, as a participant-observer, to partner with it and bring it into form.* Furthermore, nothing is predetermined in the realm of potential. For example, the potential for a dynamic new business may exist, but until you partner with that potential as a participant-observer and collapse the wave (potential) into a specific particle (form), nothing is created.

Transformational work includes helping those we serve tap into the potential (wave), perceive the possible ways the potential could be realized, and then choose one way and bring it into form (particle). Again, in a classical-physics context, we are aware of only the current reality or form. We must take that reality or form and change it into something else, if it is not to our liking. We have no choice but to work with the current reality as best we can.

In a quantum-physics context, however, we are both a participant and an observer. When something is not working, we can let the current reality (particle) dissolve back into potential (wave) to discover what other options are available or to find the missing piece. Our current circumstance or situation is only one of many possibilities. We get to choose which possibility we will partner with to cocreate a new reality.

The wave-particle principle also tells us that possibilities of the past, present, and future all exist in wave form in the quantum field. As we observe the past, we bring it into form as a particular memory. In the same way, as we observe the future, we bring it into form, cocreating the future with the wave of potential. Time is not limited to a fixed, linear path. It can also be circular (circling back on itself) or simultaneous. In addition, each participant-observer observes from a different perspective and, therefore, experiences a different reality and sequence of events.

Ervin Laszlo, recognized as the founder of systems philosophy and general evolution theory, believes that the fundamental wave-particle level of the quantum field is a holographic blueprint of the universe for all time—past, present, and future. We will talk about the holographic principle in the next chapter. For now, if we assume that Laszlo's belief is true, we should be able to access information from both the future and the past. We can remember the past, so why should we not be able to remember the future? Both are present in the quantum field.

Wave-particle theory helps us understand what is actually happening when we "remember" the future. We begin by tapping into the wave, which takes us into a simultaneous time dimension where past, present, and future coexist. As we begin to remember the future, what we are actually doing is perceiving possible wave collapses—different possible ways the wave could collapse into particle and create a specific outcome in our three-dimensional reality. Because our observance of the wave causes the collapse, we can observe many possible future outcomes in our linear-time reality, choose the one we wish to manifest, and partner with that potential to bring it into form.

We will take this principle fully into practice later in chapter 17 when we talk about the Potential-Based Approach.

Inquiry: The Participant-Observer Principle

➤ In what situations or circumstances are you acting merely as an observer? In what situations are you engaging as a participant-observer? How do your experiences and results differ depending on which approach you choose?

➤ How does your experience of life change when you shift from being only an observer to being a participant-observer?

➤ In leadership or service, what is the difference between being a participant-observer and being only an observer?

➤ How can the idea of multiple realities within the same occurrence inform your leadership or service? How might each person within a situation experience a different reality of it?

➤ How can moving from particle back into wave provide access to other options within a challenge?

Understanding Quantum Shifts

In the quantum realm, particles can jump from one orbit to another, from one reality to another. They can disappear from one place and time and reappear in another, indicating that there are multiple realities. Therefore, in the quantum realm, space and time are not smooth and continuous as they are in the three-dimensional realm. McTaggart describes quantum particles as omnipresent: "For instance, when transiting from one energy state to another, electrons seemed to be testing out all possible new orbits at once, like a property buyer attempting to live in every house on the block *at the same instant* before choosing which one to finally settle in. And nothing was certain" (*The Field*, p. 10).

You can only predict where quantum particles *might* settle into a particle state. There is no guarantee they will do so. At the most fundamental level of matter, the world and its relationships are uncertain, in a state of pure potential and infinite possibilities.

The term *quantum leap* has become a part of mainstream vocabulary in recent years, yet is rarely defined. The word *quantum* literally means "whole." When something makes a quantum leap, it jumps, whole and complete, from one reality to another. There is no sign of a pathway or how it got from one reality or position to another, nor is there a time lag. It just simultaneously disappears from one place and reappears in another.

As humans, we are capable of making quantum leaps from one belief to another, one thought to another, one behavior to another, or from one possibility to another. We are capable of instantaneous transformation if we choose it. We don't have to travel a long, circuitous route of change, consideration, and struggle. We can choose to make shifts instantaneously. Quantum shifts can occur within teams, organizations, individuals, families, and our bodies. They are limited only by our lack of belief, and even then we are sometimes caught off guard by a quantum leap that we would never have thought possible.

Inquiry: Quantum Shifts

➤ When have you experienced a quantum shift in thought, belief, or behavior, or observed such a shift in someone close to you? What do you know about how it happened?

➤ Where in your life or work would you like to make a quantum leap in thought, belief, behavior, or possibility? What would that transformation look like?

➤ What are your beliefs around the possibility of quantum shifts?

➤ How could the concept of quantum leaps inform and embolden your leadership or service?

FUNDAMENTAL PRINCIPLES OF CLASSICAL AND QUANTUM PHYSICS

CLASSICAL PHYSICS	QUANTUM PHYSICS
The physical world is real because we perceive it through our five outer senses in a three-dimensional reality. It exists whether or not anyone is observing or participating in it.	The real world exists as waves and particles rather than as solid objects. It goes in and out of physical form.
Space is fixed and absolute.	The fundamental particles of the physical world are not fixed, but instead constantly move and change. That movement and change are affected by how we observe it.
Time is linear.	Time is nonlinear.
The observer is completely separate from what is happening.	The observer is an active participant in what is happening.
Locality: objects have a specific time and space location and can be in only one location at a time.	Nonlocality: Particles do not have a specific time and space location, but instead are everywhere simultaneously.
Cause and effect can happen only in a linear time frame, and time can only move forward. Objects can only be influenced by direct contact. If objects are not in direct contact with one another, they have no impact or influence on one another.	Cause and effect does not necessarily apply. Particles that appear to be separate are actually connected by a web of energy. Physical contact is not necessary for one object to influence another.
Everything in nature flows in a continuous space-time dimension. There are no jumps in time and space.	Particles can jump from one reality to another. Therefore, time and space are not smooth and continuous. A sequence of events depends on the context and perspective of the observer. Time can be linear, circular, or simultaneous.

Traditional leadership and service have been grounded in a classical-physics paradigm. Transformational leadership and service are grounded in a quantum-physics paradigm.

CHAPTER THIRTEEN

The Quantum Field, Intuition, and Mystical Experience

If you define spirit, somewhere along the line you get a definition of something like "an invisible moving force." If I define the nature of quantum mechanics, it's an invisible moving force. So it really says, yes, there are invisible forces giving shape to our existence. . . . What quantum mechanics has put into place is that invisible moving forces are everything.

—BRUCE LIPTON, PH.D., *biologist*

Scientists don't really know what energy is; they just know that it exists, can be measured, and forms matter. Patterns of energy go together to form information. In the quantum field, information is the way that knowledge is organized. Intelligence is the measure of the ability to learn or understand from experience and to process information.

Many scientists believe that there is an inherent intelligence in the quantum field. The field and all of its components, which include all forms of life—including us—constantly process the information exchanged within the field.

At the quantum level, all objects and life-forms are vibrating fields of energy. Intermixed in that energy field is stored information that carries the history of that particular object or life-form. The ancient Eastern traditions speak of this stored information as the Akashic Records, the etheric records of all time. You might think of the Akashic Records as a massive virtual library containing all the knowledge, wisdom, and information about all that has ever been, is now, and will ever be. As we develop our intuitive senses, we find that we are increasingly able to access this information. The existence of the Akashic Records can be explained to be the result of the energetic emissions of all forms of creation. Its information is available in the quantum field, and because the information is nonlocal, it is available anytime and anywhere to those who have refined their intuitive skills to the level that they can perceive these energetic emissions. (This same concept explains such phenomena as remote viewing, the ability to tune in to and observe objects that are distant in time and space from your current physical location. For more information on remote viewing, see Jim Schnable's *Remote Viewers: The Secret History of America's Psychic Spies* and David Morehouse's *The Remote Viewing Training Course*.) Looking into the past or future involves tapping into the stored information that exists and reading its content, hearing its message, and perceiving its history.

Walter Schempp, a mathematics professor at the University of Siegen in Germany, discovered that the quantum field is a vast memory store, which led him to the theory that memory does not reside in the brain, but in the quantum field. From that discovery, scientists and theorists proposed that the brain is merely a retrieval mechanism—that it retrieves information from the quantum field (Lynne McTaggart, *The Field*, p. 95). This theory would explain how one thought or stimulus can be the catalyst for an explosion of memories, inspiration, ideas, and comprehension. It would also explain instant memory recall, the idea that we don't have to sort through a vast filing system of our own memory to locate a desired piece of information. Instead, our brains simply tap into the nonlocal quantum field and retrieve the information we need.

The theory that we are connected to the vast storehouse of information that is the quantum field takes us back to the Principle of Mentalism: THE ALL is in All, and All is in THE ALL. We each have individual minds and are individual beings existing within Consciousness. *And at the same time*, Consciousness exists within our individual minds. Consciousness is nonlocal—it does not exist in a specific time and space location, but in all time and space simultaneously. We tap into that great Consciousness for knowledge, wisdom, and understanding. Another way of saying this is that your mind exists within the quantum field, and the quantum field exists within your mind. You are a holographic image of the quantum mind/field.

We live in a holographic universe. A hologram is a pattern that is whole and complete within itself, which, at the same time, is part of a larger pattern that is whole and complete within itself, which is, in turn, a part of a larger pattern that is whole and complete, and so on. In a hologram, every part contains the essence of the whole; each piece of a holographic picture contains the essence of the entire picture.

The Principles of Mentalism and Correspondence were the ways the ancient mystery schools described what science now calls a hologram. "THE ALL is in All, and All is in THE ALL" is another way of saying "every part contains the whole," the whole being the quantum field. And "As above, so below; as below, so above" is another way of saying that anything that happens in any part of creation is immediately reflected throughout all of creation.

These emerging theories can be very challenging for us to accept on an intellectual level, because things feel very separate and distinct from us in the world that we perceive with our five outer senses. We in the Western culture have also been conditioned to believe that science and spirituality cannot coexist and, in fact, that they contradict one another to the point of being enemies. Here is the separation of the vertical and horizontal planes again. However, when we expand our awareness beyond the horizontal/rational plane into the vertical/ intuitive realm, dropping inside ourselves to the wisdom of the heart and soul, the conflict or separation between science and spirituality no longer exists. We tap into a much greater reality, where we instinctively know this "oneness of all time and space" to be true.

We tend to think of the mind as functioning in two modes: intellectual and intuitive. Generally speaking, rational thinking has been considered the realm of science, and intuitive thinking the realm of art, mysticism, and religion. The Eastern traditions have always valued intuitive thinking, while in the West, at least since the seventeenth century, intellectual and scientific knowledge have been considered the only true, credible knowledge.

Psychic and mystical experiences have been reported throughout history and in all cultures. Many laboratory experiments have attempted to explain these phenomena. These experiments continue today in places such as the Institute of Noetic Sciences Research Lab in Petaluma, California. Studies of near-death experiences have also yielded compelling evidence supporting the ideas of a consciousness and an intuitive process.

This evidence has long been controversial. However, the flexibility of time and space, nonlocality, the ability of one thing to influence another across space and time—all attributes of the quantum field—explain how psychic and mystical phenomena can happen.

The pioneering research in quantum physics in recent years is now bringing us back to an "all is one" worldview. These discoveries support many ancient spiritual traditions' universal beliefs about the nature of reality. Breakthrough research is bringing us new knowledge that transcends our mechanistic view of the world and our linear understanding of time and space. It is opening new means of understanding the mind-body connection and the relationship between Consciousness and the three-dimensional world in which we live. Many scientists, philosophers, and thought leaders, including the late David Bohm, Fritjof Capra, Amit Goswami, Gregg Braden, Edgar Mitchell, Deepak Chopra, Dean Radin, Michio Kaku, Bruce Lipton, Stephen Hawking, and Rupert Sheldrake, to name only a few, have spoken of the quantum field in ways that resemble how ancient mystics and teachers in the world's major religions spoke of God or the Creator. "Everywhere in time and space," "all knowing intelligence," "the void out of which all things come"—are we describing God or Consciousness, or the quantum field? Or are we speaking of all of them as one? One currently emerging idea is that Consciousness is the creative and sustaining force of all of creation, and that the quantum field is born out of greater Consciousness. Consciousness, therefore, is the web that connects everything in the quantum field.

If we accept that our mind is actually a field of energy that encompasses the body and the space surrounding it and that accesses the quantum field, then our conscious awareness can also expand to become one with the quantum field. What we have thought of as psychic powers or mystical experiences are actually the result of our expanded awareness into the quantum field, which has been there for us all along. It is just that we, in the Western rational-thought paradigm, have forgotten how to expand our awareness. Opening to intuitive guidance and understanding is the most real we can get, because then we are tapping into the quantum field.

Inquiry: Intuitive and Mystical Experience

➤ What new insights are you gaining into your own intuitive and mystical experiences?

➤ How can this quantum understanding of intuitive and mystical experience and energy as information inform your leadership and service?

The Technology of Miracles

Synchronicities are the coming together of things in unexpected or unplanned ways. Miracles are the results of synchronicities, usually against significant odds, at least in a three-dimensional context. Yet at the quantum level, miracles and synchronicities are simply Consciousness doing what it does. At that level, all of the components are already together in the oneness. The energetic forces (waves) are all out there in Consciousness, just waiting to be engaged (by a participant-observer, which collapses the wave into particle). What if we engaged the waves of potential? What if we accepted that our energy fields are instruments through which synchronicities and miracles can happen every day?

Through understanding and embracing the oneness of all and the function of potential (wave) coming into form (particle), we take our first step into the technology of miracles. We are not talking about magic or the supernatural. We are talking about removing anything that separates you from the miracle. When you fully embody the energetic essence of the miracle, you begin *living* the miracle. *Living* the miracle greatly increases the odds that the wave of potential will collapse into the particle of miracle in three-dimensional form.

If we accept that, on the quantum level, we are one with all that is, including the potential for what could be, then we must be one with what could be called the miraculous. Miracles are potential turned into reality, usually against powerful three-dimensional-world odds. But, as we have learned, we can choose to expand our awareness beyond what we think we know, beyond our current context, and access possibilities and potential we never knew existed. Living the miracle is not a guarantee that everything will unfold as you desire. (There are often many factors involved.) Yet when you step into and become one with what wants to happen, you accept your responsibility and claim your role in bringing potential into form.

Biologist and epistemologist Francisco Varela speaks of the state of synchronicity, miracles, and our "open nature":

> [This] is in the spiritual realm—spiritual because it has to do with human hearts. When we are in touch with our "open nature," our emptiness, we exert an enormous attraction to other human beings. There is great magnetism in that state of being which has been called . . . "authentic presence." Isn't that beautiful? And if others are in that same space or entering it, they resonate with us and immediately doors are open to us. It is not strange or mystical. It is part of the natural order.
>
> Those that are in touch with that capacity are seen as great warriors in the American Indian tradition, or as Samurai in the Eastern tradition. . . . There is great danger if we consider these people to be exceptional. They are not. This capacity is a part of the natural order and is a manifestation of something we haven't seen previously, not something we do not have. This state is available to us all, and yet it is the greatest of all human treasures.
>
> This state—where we connect deeply with others and doors open—is there waiting for us. It is like an optical illusion. All

we have to do is squint and see that it has been there all along, waiting for us. All we have to do is to see the oneness that we are (Jaworski, *Synchronicity*, pp. 179–80).

What if the miraculous were just beyond our current awareness— just inches beyond our grasp? When we embody the quantum field and become one with it, we become one with the miraculous. We *are* the miraculous, living the miraculous every moment of every day. In Peter Senge's words, "If we were not making such an immense effort to separate ourselves from life, we might actually live life day to day, minute by minute, as a series of predictable miracles" (Jaworski, *Synchronicity*, p. 14).

Inquiry: Predictable Miracles

➤ What would it mean to you personally to live your life as a series of predictable miracles?

➤ How can this understanding of miracles and synchronicity inform and empower your leadership and service?

CHAPTER FOURTEEN

The Quantum Nature of Transformational Presence

Yourself is actually the whole of mankind. That's the idea of implicate order—that everything is enfolded in everything. The entire past is enfolded in each one of us in a very subtle way. If you reach deeply into yourself, you are reaching into the very essence of mankind. When you do this, you will be led into the generating depth of consciousness that is common to the whole of mankind and that has the whole of mankind enfolded in it. The individual's ability to be sensitive to that becomes the key to the change of mankind. We are all connected. If this could be taught, and if people could understand it, we would have a different consciousness.

—DAVID BOHM, *physicist*

What do these laws of quantum physics mean for us in a solid-object world of space and time? How can they inform a next step in the evolution of personal presence? How can understanding them help us create a world that works? The more you play with these ideas and embrace the concept that, at the quantum level, things are not as they appear in the three-dimensional level, the more you are aware of multiple realities at once. There is the solid-object, three-dimensional reality that we might think of as the product or results reality, and there are quantum realities where everything is energetic potential. In this quantum reality, nothing exists as form in a specific space and time until we choose to engage it and participate with it to create something new in the three-dimensional reality. So you could think of the quantum reality as a potential/creative reality and the three-dimensional world as a fixed-form reality.

Solution-based practices in leadership and service primarily engage the three-dimensional reality, trying to change or influence fixed objects or fixed realities; sometimes these changes require huge effort and long periods of time. In transformational work, creation, planning, and guidance all begin in the potential/creative reality. When we work in the quantum world of potential and creation, nothing is fixed; everything is in wave form, just waiting for us to interact with it and create a new three-dimensional reality. The potential/creative reality then continues to be the guiding force for reaching the desired outcome in the three-dimensional, fixed-form reality.

The universe is about relationships. In physicist and systems theorist Fritjof Capra's words, "Quantum theory forces us to see the universe not as a collection of physical objects, but rather as a complicated web of relations between the various parts of a unified whole. . . . It has come to see the universe as an interconnected web of physical and mental relations whose parts are only defined through their connections to the whole" (Capra, *The Tao of Physics*, pp. 138, 141).

So it is with transformational leadership and service. There is a saying: the whole is equal to or created by the sum of its parts. However, I invite you to look at the relationship between the whole and the parts differently. In a transformational paradigm, the whole creates the parts rather than the parts creating the whole.

Creation, accomplishment, and manifestation are not about the parts by themselves; they are about the whole and the relationship of all the parts to that whole. Life and leadership involve letting the whole, or the potential for what the whole can be, inspire the parts so that they can come together to realize the potential. In this way, each of the parts contains the essence of the whole.

Working from the potential whole and the unfolding relationships between all the parts leads to amazing synchronicities. We have said that synchronicities occur because everything is connected to everything else via the quantum field. Things may appear to be random and separate, but through the intricate web of connection, everything is actually drawn together into one. All of the pieces that come together in synchronicity are connected parts of a greater whole.

Related to synchronicity is the concept of critical mass, or to use Malcolm Gladwell's term, a tipping point of thought. (Malcolm Gladwell explores many ways in which critical mass shows up in our world in his 2002 book *The Tipping Point*.) Critical mass describes what happens when a shift in consciousness, attitude, or behavior is experienced by so many people that the consciousness, attitude, or behavior of the whole population begins to shift. Those few people who initiate the shift are a part of the huge web of Consciousness that makes up the quantum field. When those few make a shift, it changes the whole, because all the people are representations of and connected to the whole. That shift in the whole happens through the holographic nature of the universe. Let's look at the holographic principle a little more deeply.

At some point in your life, you have probably stood in front of a three-way mirror in a clothing store or tailor's fitting room and seen the image of your body repeating an infinite number of times in the mirror's reflection. Using that memory as context, imagine that you are completely surrounded by mirrors—six panels around you and a mirrored floor and ceiling. The image of your body is now reflected in every direction out to infinity. This is a very simple metaphor for a holographic universe. The center object is immediately reflected out through the universe to infinity through the endless mirror reflections. Any change in the center object is immediately reflected to infinity. The image is nonlocal—it exists everywhere at once—and there is no time lag between when the change occurs in the center object and when it is reflected to infinity. The greater the number of people who reflect a specific thought, belief, or behavior out through Consciousness, the stronger that energy becomes. Eventually, the tipping point, or critical mass, is reached, and the thought, belief, or behavior of the whole population begins to shift.

The exact percentage of a population it takes to reach critical mass varies with different sources. At one time, it was considered to be 10 percent. However, in more recent studies cited by Gregg Braden, author of *The Isaiah Effect*, the number of people required to begin shifting behavior within a population was determined to be the square root of 1 percent of the population. Therefore, in a city of one million people, it only takes 100 people to begin a significant shift in the mass consciousness of the city. In *The Isaiah Effect*, Braden also cites a number of experiments showing remarkable results from mass prayer. In September 1983, studies conducted in Jerusalem showed that intentional prayer and meditation had a significant positive impact on violence there. In 1972, studies showed a statistically measurable reduction in crime in twenty-four U.S. cities when as few as 1 percent of the population engaged in a specific meditative practice (Braden, *The Isaiah Effect*, pp. 235–37).

Again, the web of Consciousness and the holographic principle explain how this tipping point can be reached. All of the people engaged in the new thought or behavior are a part of the quantum field that is held together by the web of Consciousness. Everyone in the population is connected to everyone else. Therefore, when enough people make a shift in their thinking or belief, the mass consciousness begins to shift in the same direction, because all are a part of the one.

The more exploration and experimentation continue in quantum mechanics, the more questions arise. Much of what is being presented by researchers as possibilities—especially in the relationship between the mind, thought, Consciousness, events, circumstances, and time—is still being debated by mainstream scientific thought. Yet the evidence for the existence of an infinite web of connection between all that is, and a Consciousness that is constantly creating and sustaining the quantum field, is extremely compelling. Admittedly, I am perhaps predisposed to this view of the universe because of my many years of study of the ancient mystery schools and practice in the spiritual and Consciousness realms. But, as many scholars, philosophers, and quantum theorists have stated, there is growing evidence proving that the quantum field is closely related to what the ancient sacred texts call God and I am calling Consciousness.

Through spiritual and/or introspective practices, we can reach the deep stillness within, where we can then know and experience our oneness with all that is. In that knowledge and experience, we recognize that our true nature is pure Consciousness, the creating and sustaining force of all. And when we stand in Transformational Presence, it is in this quantum field and pure-Consciousness space that we live, create, and work in order to realize our greatest personal potential and the greatest potential for those we serve.

Exploration: The Holographic Principle at Work

Bring to your awareness a project in your life or work. Consider this project from the perspective of the present-moment reality, where the project has yet to be completed. Imagine the steps that you will probably have to take in order to accomplish your goal. Imagine each step standing on its own—one piece that, when joined together with others, you hope will lead to the outcomes you desire. Notice how it feels to consider the steps as building blocks that you hope will eventually lead to success.

Now take a few deep breaths and shake out that energy from your body. Then move to another spot in the room or change your physical position. From this new position, imagine your project as completed and successful. Feel the energy of the completed project. How would you describe it? What has happened as a result of the project being completed? You are standing in the energy of the completed whole.

Remaining in that energy, ask the project to show you the steps that led to its completion. Ask it to show you how you got there, who was involved, where the resources came from, the order of the steps you took. Notice how it feels to work from the completed whole, letting the whole create the steps. How is this different from creating the parts one at a time as separate building blocks? How can you approach other projects by letting the completed whole create each step?

Taking this idea further, consider the eight-sided mirror and the holographic principle. What would be the difference between placing the energy of the completed project in the middle instead of the energy of the individual steps you might take to get to an end result?

CHAPTER FIFTEEN

Life as an Open System

We cannot underestimate our individual and collective power
to consciously "provoke" our system's transformation in the
direction we desire; shared intention and collective purpose
drive system innovation and transformation.
—STEPHANIE PAGE MARSHALL, PH.D.

Physicists describe our quantum universe as open and insubstantial,
meaning that the universe is made up of matter in motion and,
therefore, fundamentally has no substance or definitive solid form. It
is constantly shifting, transforming, becoming. As we move from the
quantum realm toward the three-dimensional realm, things start to
become substantial in nature. They take on density, mass, and form.
How quickly, slowly, or obviously that change occurs is relative to the
density and mass of the matter.

For example, a thought has no density or mass, so our thoughts
can shift quickly. However, a paradigm or belief is a thought that has
become anchored in our energetic structure. Therefore, the time and
focus necessary to shift that belief depends on how deeply it is embed-
ded in the physical and emotional structure of our life and how complex
and layered that structure is. A belief or habit that has been reinforced
on many levels over a lifetime is likely more challenging to shift than a
belief you adopted last year or a habit you adopted last month.

Another consideration is the number of people involved in the shift.
Individuals can experience transformation and effect change in their
lives relatively quickly, if they are open and willing to transform. In

a small business, it might take somewhat longer, yet when only a few people and/or systems are involved, transformation can still occur in a relatively short period of time. On the other hand, it is probably going to take much longer for transformation to move through an entire multinational corporation because of the great numbers of people, systems, and cultures involved.

If we move back to the quantum realm and work with the business or multinational corporation at the level at which it is open and insubstantial, theoretically, transformation and change can happen much more quickly. In fact, at the quantum level, the shift is nonlocal, so it happens everywhere instantaneously. Coming from a classical, three-dimensional perspective, understanding this would require a significant paradigm leap. But what if we could go to the quantum level to effect change and, therefore, experience the result of that change immediately?

Making changes and experiencing their results would, of course, be much easier if everyone in the organization were skilled at reading energy, shifting paradigms, and creating change at the quantum level. What if leaders today were to help everyone they serve *experience* working at the quantum level, and then help those they serve develop these quantum skills to use in day-to-day operations? How would companies, organizations, communities, and governments operate differently? What could be accomplished when all decisions, policies, and actions were made from this quantum awareness?

The human family is an open system. Like everything else, we are made up of matter in motion—vibrating energy—and are, therefore, insubstantial. Anything that happens to one of us impacts all of us on some level. Anything that happens to one organization impacts all organizations. Because of the quantum web of connection between all members of the human family and all organizations or cultures, the experiences of anyone or any group are nonlocal. Consciously or subconsciously, we all share every experience that any one of us has. The more expanded our awareness, the more conscious recognition we can have of a nonlocal experience that has come through one, yet impacts all.

If we are all connected via this quantum web, then we have choices about how we relate to one another. Doc Childre, founder of the Institute of HeartMath in Boulder Creek, California, speaks of higher-heart and lower-heart feelings and responses. (For more information on the Institute of HeartMath and higher and lower heart, see *The HeartMath Solution*, pp. 42–45.) While both come out of a feeling of love, a desire to help, and a concern for the well-being of others, a lower-heart response can easily turn into excessive sympathy and unhealthy caretaking. This response can result in giving more energy to the challenge than to its resolution and can hold people captive within the challenge. A higher-heart response, on the other hand, turns the love and desire for well-being into compassion and action. It empowers individuals to push on through the situation in a way that allows the greatest potential to unfold. When responding from the high heart, you are able to feel what someone else is feeling while remaining grounded in your own authenticity.

A high-heart response offers courage and support, calling all parties to their greatest potential within the situation. Lower-heart responses offer sympathy and tend to nurture dependence. A lower-heart perspective pulls you into empathy and sympathy, while the higher heart calls you to be the compassionate observer, the voice of wisdom and clarity. Lower-heart engagement easily leads to an unconscious reaction to a situation, while high-heart engagement more often leads to a consciously aware response.

The high-heart energy center is located in the upper-sternum area, midway between the center of your chest and the base of your neck. The low-heart center is located just below the center of your chest and just above your solar plexus. Many people can experience the difference between these two energies simply by taking in several breaths, first through one center, then through the other. Take a few moments for the following Exploration and experience the difference for yourself.

Exploration: High Heart and Low Heart

A word of introduction: When I speak of high-heart or low-heart breaths, I am not speaking of a shallow breath and a deeper breath.

Instead, I am speaking of the energy center that is activated through the intake of the breath. Throughout the exercise, when you are working with both the low heart and high heart, your breath should be as deep and full as you can manage.

Close your eyes and take deep and full breaths, filling your entire body with air. After a few breaths, continue this breathing and imagine the breath coming in through your low-heart center, down around the base of your sternum, midway between the center of your chest and your solar plexus, and then going out through the solar plexus. Notice how it feels to activate the low-heart center through your breath. What is your physical and emotional response?

After a few moments, shift your focus to imagine the breath coming in through your high-heart center, in the upper-sternum area, midway between the center of your chest and the base of your neck, and then going out through the solar plexus. Continue taking deep and full breaths. Just shift where you imagine the air entering—the energy center you are activating. Notice again your physical and emotional response.

For most people, the high-heart breath feels more open and expansive, while breathing in through the low-heart center feels more restrictive. However, if you are accustomed to living in low-heart energy, the low-heart breath may feel more comfortable simply because living in the low heart is your habit.

In the next few days, pay attention to how you habitually approach situations in your life. Do you default to a low-heart or high-heart breath? This practice will heighten your awareness, so that the next time you find yourself in a challenging situation, you can make clear choices. The moment you feel yourself being swept up into the drama, consciously activate your high-heart center while filling your entire body with breath. Breathe all the way to your toes, and then exhale through your solar plexus. Continue that breathing pattern for several minutes, and you will feel yourself get calmer and feel your perspective shift. The high-heart breath can help you shift out of the Drama level of engagement and into Choice and Opportunity.

This breathing technique can help you gain clarity and peace in the face of most challenges. I'm not claiming it is a magical solution— "All you have to do is think nice thoughts and breathe into the magic spot, and everything will be fine." But it can be a very powerful place to begin. Research at the Institute of HeartMath overwhelmingly confirms the value of this simple technique.

As individuals, we are at different levels of mental, emotional, and spiritual awareness. Our individual levels of awareness are reflected in vibrational frequencies. A narrow range of awareness, such as that represented in self-centeredness, with no concern or thought for anyone or anything else, is reflected in a lower vibrational frequency. A greatly expanded awareness of how all of life is interconnected and interdependent is reflected in a much higher vibrational frequency. The frequencies of our individual awareness come together to form the overall vibrational frequency of the mass consciousness. Whether we are aware of it or not, and whether or not it is our intent, each one of us is an active participant in the cocreation of our mass consciousness. Although we are conditioned to see ourselves as separate from one another, from events, and from the many things that make up our world, the quantum reality is that we live in a web of relationships between all parts of creation, and those parts—and, therefore, the relationships between them—are constantly shifting and changing.

Transformational Presence calls us beyond our concept of relationship as an energy or connection between two separate entities. Since at the quantum level, everything is simply one great vibrating energy field, there are no more "us" and "them." There are no "our problems" and "their problems"—all problems are our problems, as are all our victories, all our successes, and all our challenges. At the quantum level, the entire cosmos is vibrating energy—energy in motion—and everything affects everything else. Everything is contained within the greater whole, and the greater whole contains everything.

The Principle of Correspondence says, "As above, so below; as below, so above." Through this holographic process, that principle is active in families, communities, organizations, corporate structures, nations, and the world. Individuals within a group are constantly broadcasting their state of being to the people and situations around them, whether or not they are aware they are doing so.

This brings us back to the greater understanding of "once and for *all*," discussed in chapter 3. As each of us learns, changes, and makes choices and decisions, each of us becomes a bridge for others to follow to reach new levels of Consciousness awareness. We create a change in the pattern, and as enough people create that change, the hologram changes. It is through this process that critical mass is reached. If we return to our example of standing in the middle of the mirrors (chapter 14), we see that when one person makes a shift, that shift is reflected or broadcast in every direction out to infinity. When a number of people are broadcasting the same shift, the message is intensified, making a greater impression on the mass consciousness. When enough people have broadcast a particular shift in thought and behavior, a tipping point is reached, and it leads to an entire segment of society shifting its thought and behavior. As you and those you serve make a conscious shift in your thought and behavior, you open the door for others to do the same.

At the same time, the group consciousness is broadcasting back to the individuals. The individual or group emitting the strongest broadcast signal will be the most effective in influencing others. And what makes a broadcast signal strong? Energy, focus, and intent on the part of the individual or group. This concept will be further explored in chapters 17 through 20, which discuss creating and sustaining reality fields.

Through this holographic process, the states of balance and harmony in our bodies and in the earth mirror each other. When we live in a state of inner conflict, anger, and dis-ease, we broadcast a corresponding vibrational frequency. On the other hand, when we live in a state of inner peace, resolution, and clarity of purpose and intention in alignment with soul, we reflect a very different vibrational frequency. Earthquakes, volcanic eruptions, and shifts in weather patterns may reflect the great shifts occurring in human consciousness, or they may be a response to a need for a shift. At the same time, our inner states of being are reflections of what is going on in our outer world. Note the difference in how you feel internally between when you are in the hustle and bustle of a big city and when you are watching a sunset over the ocean or sitting beside a peaceful mountain stream. These settings have very different energy vibrations and will call forth different responses and feelings from you. The holographic universe and the Principle of Correspondence are constantly in action.

Inquiry: Open Universe

➤ What does the concept of living in an open universe mean for your life and work? How might you live more fully in the awareness of all that an open universe implies?

➤ Name some specific ways that understanding the concept of an open universe could help us create a world that works.

CREATING
NEW REALITIES

CHAPTER SIXTEEN

Evolutionary Consciousness

As a man who has devoted his whole life to the most clear
headed science, to the study of matter, I can tell you as the
result of my research about the atoms this much:
"There is no matter as such!"
All matter originates and exists only by virtue of a force
which brings the particles of an atom to vibration and holds
this most minute solar system of the atom together. . . . We
must assume behind this force the existence of a conscious
and intelligent mind. This mind is the matrix of all matter.

—MAX PLANCK, *physicist*

Evolutionary consciousness refers to the unfolding of our awareness of Consciousness into ever broader and heretofore unseen
or unrecognized concepts, as well as the continued evolution of Consciousness itself. Because everything is interconnected, as we evolve in
our awareness and our ability to plumb the depths of Consciousness,
Consciousness responds to that interaction with its own continuing
evolution. As Consciousness and our awareness of it unfold, we discover new contexts for understanding and perception. This discovery,
once again, requires our willingness to expand beyond intellect.

Before we dig deeper into evolutionary Consciousness, it's important to create some shared meaning around key terms. At the beginning of this journey, I defined Consciousness as the matrix of energy
that is the creative and sustaining force of the universe, of everything
that exists in physical and nonphysical form. It is the unseen force

that Max Planck spoke of in the quote at the beginning of this chapter; it is the "intelligent mind" that is the "matrix of all matter." It is also the realm of possibility and potential. Consciousness is the force behind creation. It is the web that connects everything to everything else. And based on my understanding of ancient teachings and modern quantum physics, I believe you could also call it Love, God, Universal Mind, Intelligence, or Spirit.

Deepak Chopra refers to Consciousness as the inner intelligence of the body and of creation. He defines both Consciousness and God as a field of awareness made up of "nonlocal, acausal, quantum mechanical interrelatedness." Consciousness is everywhere in time and space. As the fundamental source of all, it is not caused by anything else; therefore, it is the one exception to the Principle of Cause and Effect. It is a field of energy in which literally everything is, in some way, connected to and impacted by everything else. Chopra explains further that everything is Consciousness differentiated into unique forms; that Consciousness, as the single reality, differentiates into thoughts, feelings, awareness, perceptions, and physical forms. Differentiation does not imply separation, but different manifestations of a source energy. (From the *Shift in Action* member audio program of the Institute of Noetic Sciences, Autumn 2005.)

This understanding of differentiation versus separation is critical in Transformational Presence work. "Everything is energy" means that every object, person, thought, and belief is made up of vibrating energy. Therefore, creation is one big mass of vibrating energy. Yet that energy differentiates into many distinct and unique forms, creating the appearance of separate things. For the sake of daily interaction with others and our environment, we operate in a paradigm that says things are separate from one another. Yet when we work from the field of potential, we must become comfortable with the *coexistence* of oneness and differentiation. "All is one" is the reality at the quantum level; differentiation is the reality in the three-dimensional realm. And both realities exist at the same time in the same space.

Consciousness is the source energy. It's not something we develop, but the energy from which we are created. We live within it, and it lives within us. Again, we see the Principles of Mentalism and Correspondence. What we develop is our *awareness* of Consciousness, our ability to access it at deeper and higher levels, and ultimately, we experience our oneness with it. As we evolve in our awareness of Consciousness, Consciousness itself evolves. Consciousness experiences itself through us, and through that experience, it continues to evolve and create itself.

The word *evolution* refers to a directionally unfolding, step-by-step process of formation, development, and growth. To say that something is evolutionary means that it is a result of a directional unfolding process, while, at the same time, it continues as a process.

It is very easy to get caught in the box of our current awareness and context, unable to see beyond our present three-dimensional reality. When this happens, we have very little chance of perceiving and understanding what is evolving within and around us. We may have no context for it or language to describe it. However, when we are able to expand beyond our contextual perceptions and understanding, we can become active participants in the evolution of both our awareness and of Consciousness itself. At this point, we truly become cocreators with Consciousness and potential, rather than being limited to what we can create within our current reality.

As our awareness evolves, we continue to uncover new levels of Consciousness, revealing new seeds of potential and allowing them to grow in ways they never could before. As we evolve, potential evolves, and as we discover more about that evolving potential, we evolve. Life becomes an extraordinary dance of new discovery and understanding meeting new potential, meeting new discovery and understanding, meeting new potential, meeting new discovery and understanding—and on it goes.

The Matrix of Consciousness

Transformational work calls us to engage in and serve the evolution of human awareness and of Consciousness itself. Quantum physicists continue to discover ways in which we are all interconnected through the Consciousness matrix. We live the paradox of being separate, unique, and differentiated individuals who are, at the same time, one interconnected being through the matrix of Consciousness. In our separateness, we make choices, and because of the holographic nature of the matrix of Consciousness, our individual choices affect the whole.

Let's explore the matrix of Consciousness experientially. Take a few minutes for the following exercise.

Exploration: The Web of Consciousness

Close your eyes and focus your attention on your breath. Take a few moments to allow your breath to find its own natural, steady, even rhythm. When you have reached a place of inner stillness and quiet, continue with the exercise. Let go of any preconceived notion about whether or not you know how to do what the exercise asks, and trust that somewhere within your awareness, you do. Let go of any preconceived idea of what your experience will or should be. Just be with whatever happens.

In your imagination, float up and out of your body about 100 feet above where you are now. Float here for a few moments, and begin to perceive or imagine the strands of the web of energy between you and others with whom you share your space, and between you and the space itself. Allow your intuitive senses to experience the energy.

Now continue to rise higher, floating up above your city. Pause here for a few moments to give yourself time to perceive the web of energy in the city. Then float up above your region of the country. As the web expands, how do you perceive it? Continue floating higher until you can see the curve of the earth. How do you perceive the web of energy that exists between all aspects of creation? You may perceive strands of energy between people, between people and places, and even between people on earth and people in the spirit world. If you continue to float farther out into the universe, you may also perceive strands of energy between planets, stars, moons, and celestial bodies. This is the matrix of Consciousness.

What new awareness is unfolding for you through this exercise? How are you perceiving our world differently? What differences do you feel physically, emotionally, and spiritually? How might your life be different if you remained aware of this matrix throughout your day?

When you are ready, take time to write your thoughts in your journal.

Synchronicity

We have established that the universe is completely interconnected through the matrix of Consciousness. Everything emerges out of this interconnectedness. Our thoughts and ideas are energy. The more attention we give to those thoughts and the clearer our intent, the more those thoughts and ideas move out into the Consciousness web. Within that web, the universe responds, and pieces begin to fall into place.

When we experience the matrix of Consciousness, we can begin to understand how synchronicity works. Synchronicity occurs because everything is connected. The connections may appear to be random, but it is through an intricate web of ordered connection that everything is drawn together into one. All of the pieces that fall into place synchronistically are actually connected parts of a greater whole.

Intel senior officer David Marsing says, "Synchronicity is about being open to what wants to happen" (quoted in Peter Senge et al., *Presence: Human Purpose and Field of Potential*, p. 164). We have defined Consciousness as intelligence. Many would argue that there is an intelligence guiding the evolutionary process and, therefore, an intelligence guiding unfolding potential. If we pay attention, we can tap into that intelligence and begin to perceive the signs of that unfolding potential; we can perceive what wants to happen. The more we open to the wave of the quantum field, tap into the intelligence that creates and sustains that field, and ask for and align with what wants to happen as the greatest potential of the moment or situation, the more synchronicities occur.

We sometimes view synchronicities as weird occurrences—sometimes so weird that we hesitate to tell anyone else about them. But again, what if synchronicities—and miracles—are simply Consciousness doing what it does? What if synchronicities and miracles are natural states of being and natural occurrences in Consciousness?

Thinking of synchronicity and miracles this way may be new to you. On the other hand, you might say, "Of course, I know this." But do you live it? Do you *expect* miracles and synchronicities as a part of Consciousness in creation? Do you live and work in this way of thinking all the time? What if your body and energy field are instruments through which miracles and synchronicities are waiting to occur every day?

It can be easy to dismiss this idea as pretty far-fetched. But just for the sake of wonder and possibility, really consider these inquiries. What if we were to let the potential show us a picture, step into the energetic essence of what brought that picture into being, and follow the energy through to its creation? What if we were to let go of our need to be in control of the creative process and let *what wants to unfold* do its magic? What if our job was to respond to what wants to happen rather than to *make* something happen in the way we think it should?

We are one with Consciousness. We are one with the quantum field. Living in this awareness, we can also be one with the miraculous and, in fact, can live miracles and synchronicities every day. Imagine what life would look like from this place! Imagine how differently we would "create" our lives and projects. Imagine how our action plans would be different. What would *your* life and work look like if you consciously lived in the space of miracles and synchronicity? Imagine if living in miracles and synchronicity were the standard approach to leadership, business, and government. In these rapidly changing and transformational times, we have the choice to either rocket into new dimensions of possibilities and partner with them for creation, or to stand in the smoke of what once was, but is no longer.

CHAPTER SEVENTEEN

The Potential-Based Approach

You never change things by fighting the existing reality. To change something, build a new model that makes the existing model obsolete.

—BUCKMINSTER FULLER, *inventor and futurist*

Our universe is made up of matter in motion. It is constantly shifting, changing, and becoming. How quickly, slowly, or obviously that change occurs is relative to the density and mass of the form, organization, or situation. The more density, the slower the vibrational frequency. The larger the form or the more complex the organization or situation, the longer it can take for change to permeate it.

How quickly or slowly, efficiently or inefficiently, we are able to implement change depends on whether we are working with it in form or in potential. When we work in form, change is a slow process. Compared to pure energy and potential, form is a heavier, less pliable energy. However, the pure energy of potential is very flexible and easy to work with. Therefore, when we work in energetic potential, change can happen much more rapidly. Working with potential means becoming the three-dimensional partner that potential needs to be realized in form. In the same way that we need potential to be the source of inspiration, creativity, and innovation, potential needs us to be a grounding force to help it manifest in the three-dimensional realm. By partnering with potential, we become active participants in the cocreation of our present and our future.

Energy is the key. When we keep our focus on the energy, the potential remains alive and informs every step taken, every new form created. However, when we focus on only the form or are attached to a specific outcome, the true potential may never be realized. We get stuck in the vibrational frequency of the form we have chosen. Einstein has been quoted many times as having said, "Problems cannot be solved by the same level of thinking that created them." When we are focused on solving a problem, we remain stuck in the level of consciousness of the problem, regardless of our good intentions. When we shift our focus to the potential, we move to a higher level of vibrational frequency and are no longer locked in former patterns and contexts. In this new frequency, we can give energy to a new creation, to the potential that the problem has helped us see. In the new frequency, there is a much better chance for the greatest potential to emerge and for us to follow that energy toward a new reality.

Most people associate potential and possibilities with the future, with something to be attained down the road, often after a lot of other things have been accomplished or fallen into place. However, if we go back to the quantum reality, where past, present, and future all coexist, we find that the potential and possibilities we had perceived for the future actually exist right now. In the quantum field, they are all present all the time.

The holographic principle tells us that all of the parts contain the essential elements of the whole. Who you are right now contains the seeds—all the essential elements—for who you can become. The seeds of your full potential are already planted within you. The challenge is to continue growing and expanding in awareness, so that you can discover the seeds, water them, and thus lead them to germinate.

The same is true for those that you serve. The seeds of their greatest potential lie within them right now. Our job as transformation workers is to support their awakening to higher and higher levels of awareness, so that they are able to perceive the unfolding potential for themselves, their colleagues, and their organizations. The possible ways that potential might manifest are many. Our job is to call potential and possibility into this three-dimensional realm. And we do that through a process we call the Potential-Based Approach.

The Four Principles of the Potential-Based Approach

The Potential-Based Approach brings together all of the concepts, understanding, and tools we have been exploring into a simple leadership and service model. Transformational Presence makes the implementation of this model possible. It is grounded in four of the fundamental principles that we have already explored.

1. Everything is energy.

This is the fundamental law of the universe. At the most basic level, everything is energy in vibration and, therefore, has an energetic essence. Through quantum theory, we understand that until energy takes a specific form, it has the potential to become anything. In the Potential-Based Approach we go straight to pure essence energy; discover the greatest potential waiting to unfold through a particular situation, project, or goal; and partner with that potential to bring it to reality. We create at the level of energetic essence, where form flows out of potential, rather than potential being limited by a preconceived form.

2. Expanded awareness opens the door to potential.

Throughout this book, you have been introduced to concepts and practices designed to help you live in an ever-expanding field of awareness. This expanded awareness opens the door to your greatest potential and the greatest potential of a situation, project, or organization. In expanded awareness, you become aware of many levels of reality at the same time and can draw on those various levels for the skills, tools, and knowledge you need in the present moment.

3. Potential leads the way.

The Potential-Based Approach explores new frontiers of who we are as human beings. Instead of viewing potential as belonging to the future, as something to aspire to, what if we could live our potential now? What if we called it from the future into the present?

The Potential-Based Approach explores what it means for each of us to live our greatest personal potential now instead of waiting for later. From there, we can tap into the greatest potential for a project, situation, or circumstance and, ultimately, for humanity. As we tap into the potential, it begins to guide us toward its full realization. Traditionally, we are trained to learn from the past. The past certainly has a lot to teach us, and it is important to be aware of where we have been and of what we and those before us have learned. Yet the future can be our teacher as well. It can show us what is possible and then show us the path to it.

4. We must close the gaps between what we know and how we live.

For most of us, regardless of our level of awareness, there remain gaps between what we know and how we live. Each of us must ask ourselves on a regular basis, "Am I living what I know? Are those I serve living what they know?" Without this fourth principle, the first three will not take us very far.

This principle brings us to the concepts of practice and praxis. Praxis is the integration of your belief with your behavior. Practice is how you get to praxis. If your knowledge remains only an intellectual understanding of concepts, then your presence may be informational or transactional, but it will not be transformational.

Closing the gaps can catapult you to vast new levels of awareness in consciousness and create and develop your presence. From there, how you live, work, relate, lead, serve, and create evolves. When you *live* from your vast knowledge, intuition, wisdom, and soul, your understanding of life and your ability to play with that understanding expand exponentially. The time that it takes you to go from learning and understanding to practical application gets shorter and shorter. You *live* your evolving knowledge and understanding. This is the essence of Transformational Presence.

Although we will talk further about closing the gaps and practice and praxis in chapter 21, take time for this Inquiry to begin applying this principle now.

Inquiry: Close the Gap

As you continue applying all you have learned, be acutely aware of the places where your current way of living—your habits, choices, thoughts, and beliefs—are out of alignment with what you know or claim to be true and possible. Where do you know one thing and live another? Where do you espouse an ideal, yet not live it in your daily life? Bring your life into complete alignment with your knowledge and personal truths. Close the gap between what you know and how you live.

In leadership and service, calling those you serve to close gaps can require speaking uncomfortable truths. How well do you help those you serve align behavior with belief, action with personal values and truth? How well do you speak and remain fully present with uncomfortable truth? The level of transformational power and strength in personal presence is, in large part, dependent on the level of alignment and congruence between behavior and belief, between action and values, between decisions and the greater potential, between choices and the soul essence.

The Parts Are Creations of the Whole

In the Potential-Based Approach, we let energetic potential create components and lead the way. Our conditioned beliefs of the past, rooted in the concepts of classical physics and the idea that everything is separate from everything else, told us that the whole is made up of the sum of its parts. In that paradigm, the parts come first, and we can get very busy working on the parts, thinking that they will somehow come together and create a whole. Yet, as discussed in chapter 14, quantum physics tells us something different: *the parts are created by the whole*—the holographic model. The Potential-Based Approach brings this concept into full focus for leadership and service. In the Potential-Based Approach, we let the potential guide the creation and manifestation of anything we're working on.

The bodies of most life-forms are great examples of the whole creating the parts. Each body forms out of a single cell, which contains the DNA, or the essence, of the entire body. That first cell contains all that is needed to create the whole. That cell then divides, and those cells divide. The process continues, as cells divide and multiply and become differentiated to perform the functions of particular organs and body parts. But every cell and resulting body part contains the DNA, the essence, of the entire body. Every cell knows its relationship to all other cells and to the whole because it was created from a cell containing the whole.

Allowing the whole to create the parts is paralleled in transformational leadership and service. As we create something new or start work on a new project, we must discover the potential in the whole and then create each part from that potential. When we start a project from the perspective of the completed whole, the whole will be present in every part. We tap into the energetic essence of that which is wanting to happen, the potential waiting to unfold, and let it guide us. Then every step, every component, is filled with and created by the potential. Every component or part is holographic in nature. Our job as transformational leaders is to ensure that each new step along the way contains the essence of the whole.

Potential, Possibility, and Outcome

The words *potential* and *possibility* are often used interchangeably. However, in the Potential-Based Approach, we make a clear distinction between them. Potential is often thought to be a specific result that could happen in the future. However, in the Potential-Based Approach, potential is seen as an energetic essence present right now and wanting to emerge. Potential is the energy of creation not yet in

---

POTENTIAL = an energetic essence; energy waiting to take form; what wants to happen

---

POSSIBILITY = a form that the potential might take in the physical realm; energy taking a specific form; what could happen

---

OUTCOME = the form has taken shape and become "real" in the physical realm; what did happen

form. Potential has movement and action. It is an energetic cause that creates an effect. Potential is *what is waiting and wanting to happen*. Possibility is a specific way that the potential might manifest into form. It is *what could happen*. Outcome, then, represents the end result—how it all turned out, *what did happen*.

Suppose a company wants to launch a new product. In an old paradigm, it starts with the outcome, launching the product, in mind; considers the possibilities of promotional campaigns to get the product out there; and then considers what potential might emerge once the project has been launched. If the new product gets launched and its success matches what the company had hoped for, everyone is pleased.

Using the Potential-Based Approach, however, the company might discover that instead of just launching a product, the greatest potential waiting to unfold is the market opening to a new way of thinking about an entire genre of products. The possible means (the possibilities) of opening the market include promotional campaigns, a new product design, public-education campaigns, and perhaps a repositioning of the company brand. The outcome, then, is an entirely different line of new products and a whole new look and feel for the company. When the company started, it was not clear what the outcome would be, except that, at a minimum, it would get the new product launched. By focusing on the potential instead of the outcome, so much more happened.

Potential, possibility, and outcome are all parts of a creation equation. Regardless of what we might want to create, we are conditioned to start with a specific outcome in mind and then push to make it happen. While an outcome does provide important focus and direction, it can also trap us in a fixed form with fixed conditions. In addition, it can put us in problem-solving mode, in which we give more energy to our current circumstance than to what the true potential might be.

As an example of the problem-solving approach in action, consider a community that is having a problem with teen violence and gang warfare. The conventional problem-solving approach to this situation would be to try to figure out how to stop the violence. In order to reach that outcome, community leaders consider possibilities, such as tightly controlling teen activities and associations so that young people have fewer opportunities to get involved in gangs. The leaders might try creating stiffer legal penalties and jail sentences, establishing and enforcing curfews, and increasing police presence within the community. From these possibilities, they would say that the potential is reduced violence, gangs broken up and stripped of their power on the street, and people in the community feeling safer. They would spend tremendous energy figuring out solutions and trying to make things happen. Even if the potential were reached—the violence stopped—there is a good chance that the solution would only be temporary. The question "What is the greatest potential here?" would never have been asked.

However, there is another way the community could approach the challenge: the Potential-Based Approach. Acknowledging the current reality of teen violence and gang warfare, the leaders could ask, "In the greatest potential of this circumstance, what is wanting to happen?" They could tap into that potential and ask it to show them the possible ways it could be realized. Once they see the possibilities, they can choose the one or more they feel the most drawn to and partner with those possibilities to create a new outcome.

Suppose they discover that the *potential* is to inspire teenagers to become community leaders and to have a stake in their community's life. *Possibilities* for giving that potential form could include the development of an after-school life-purpose and leadership program for teens, a multigenerational travel-study program for learning how other cultures create community, or a new community-awareness and civics curriculum within the school program. A new *outcome* could be not only a significant drop in violence, but also the young people having a sense of community ownership and purpose, and people from multiple generations engaging in ongoing dialogue. What a different atmosphere could be created than if they had just focused on stopping the violence!

The problem-solving approach begins with the current situation and tries to figure out some possible solutions. In that approach, potential usually means that the problem gets solved, and we're happy with that. However, no real forward movement has happened. We've just fixed a problem. We've remained in the Drama and Situation levels of engagement.

The Potential-Based Approach starts by going straight to the Opportunity level and asking, "What wants to happen here? What is the gift of this situation? What is this situation really trying to help us see?" As we perceive the potential—what wants to happen—we ask it to intuitively show us all possible means for realizing that potential. We then focus on the possibilities that really speak to us, and we partner with them to bring the potential into reality. The outcome is discovered in the process. In the end, instead of just solving a problem, we've created a new reality. We have moved forward in our evolution and development.

Let's look at another example to see the Potential-Based Approach at work. The McArthur family needed a new house. They had three children, two dogs, and multiple family interests. Their present house was a rental, too small, and not close enough to good schools. They could afford only $2,000 a month in mortgage payments and taxes, and they had only $30,000 in cash for a down payment. They realized that buying a house was going to be a stretch, but they set about trying to figure out how to make it work. They considered various financing options, met with several real estate agents, and began pushing to make the new house happen within the limitations of their current circumstance. Very quickly, they became discouraged, because they were told that the kind of house they wanted did not exist in their area within their price range. It seemed that they

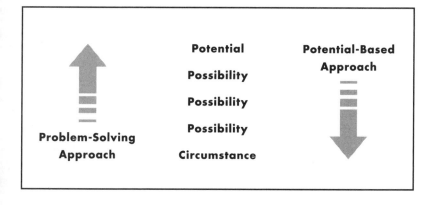

might have to move to another area, which would mean new schools and long commutes to work. Obstacles kept appearing, and it seemed that each challenge led to ten others.

After struggling for several months, the McArthurs decided to try the Potential-Based Approach. Abandoning their preconceived notion of what they thought they needed, they began exploring the greatest potential of this situation from a more expanded awareness. They discovered that what wanted to happen was family members each having space to pursue their individual creative interests and, at the same time, family members bonding by undertaking a project together. Having the optimal spaces for individual creative interests and a family project were not even considerations before. While the practicalities of good schools and financial parameters were still in the mix, they chose to focus on the individual and collective potential for their family. With this perspective, the situation began to feel more open, and they breathed more easily. They had lifted out of problem-solving and into new creation.

Letting the potential of more creative space and family bonding guide them, they contacted a new real estate agent and began a new search. She showed them a house in a nearby neighborhood that they hadn't even considered because of its reputation for high prices. However, because this particular house needed some updating and cosmetic improvements and had been tied up in the settling of an estate, the heirs were anxious to sell the house quickly and had drastically reduced the price. The house had just the right kinds of spaces for each family member to pursue his or her own interests. There was a large, fenced-in back yard for the dogs, and very good schools were less than a mile away. Furthermore, by working together, the family could make most of the needed improvements themselves, which would create an opportunity for bonding. Suddenly, a new reality had been created. The McArthurs bought and settled into the new house that met all of their individual needs, and they remained within their budget. And as the whole family joined together to make the needed home improvements, they developed great pride around what they had created together.

We do not evolve by solving problems. Solving problems keeps us trapped in an old model of potential limited to our current context and situation. We evolve by partnering with unlimited potential and creating new realities. The problems then become irrelevant, take care of themselves, or disappear. They simply do not exist within the new reality.

The Potential-Based Approach is a process of emergence. It is about creating new realities based on the greatest potential. As we partner with the potential and let it show us the way toward its manifestation, outcomes emerge that are often far beyond what we originally imagined.

Acknowledging What Is

Working with the Potential-Based Approach does not mean that we deny current circumstances. It is important that we acknowledge *what is* right here, right now. However, acknowledging a circumstance does not mean that we need to keep feeding it energy. That is an important distinction. By acknowledging the "what is," and our role in creating the conditions that gave birth to and continue to support that present circumstance, we are empowered to create something different. Yet choosing or creating a new reality in the face of difficult circumstances can be incredibly daunting.

There are many examples of difficult and even horrific circumstances in the world. However, when we acknowledge that yes, indeed, this is our current circumstance—no matter how difficult or horrific it is—and then focus our energy toward creating a new circumstance, we move toward freedom. Jane Goodall, the pioneering chimpanzee researcher and now an environmental activist, is a living example of this concept. Each time I hear her speak or read something she has written, I am struck by her ability to remain focused on the potential. She speaks of the "what is," laying out the facts about the rapid extinction of record numbers of species and endangerment of life as we know it on planet earth with a calm yet sobering voice. She offers no criticism or blame, gives no energy to how we got to where we are—she simply makes a clear statement of the current reality. Her voice is soft, yet her energy shakes the rafters as she speaks of little-known individuals and groups who are busy creating a different reality. She speaks of the world we can create for our grandchildren's grandchildren and of exactly how we can do it as she shares one story after another of how it is already being done. She gives no energy to solving problems, but rather invites us to a tipping point, where the mass consciousness focuses on creating optimal conditions that can allow a new reality to take hold.

Goodall acknowledges the present circumstance *and* focuses on the potential. We get to choose our relationship to our present circumstance—to the "what is." We can choose to acknowledge the circumstance, take the immediate steps necessary to shift the situation out of crisis, and then focus on what is being called for in the greatest potential that wants to unfold.

If people are starving, we take immediate steps to feed them, and then as quickly as possible, focus our energies on tapping into the bigger picture of what is being called for. Perhaps the greater potential is hearts opening to a new level. Perhaps it is skill-building among the starving population once the people are strong enough to support themselves. Perhaps it is a new set of priorities for government. What is the big picture?

If someone you serve is in a precarious financial situation, you help him or her take immediate steps to keep afloat, and at the same time, become aware of and focus on the true message in the challenge. Perhaps the true potential for growth is in a different direction. What is the underlying message? How can that message help you lead him or her to the greatest potential of the situation?

Inquiry: Approaching What Is

➤ What is the "what is" in a situation in your life? Are you approaching it from circumstance or potential? What is the gift?

➤ Consider a "what is" for an individual or organization you serve. What breakthrough is waiting to happen? How can you help that individual or organization make that breakthrough?

Leading and serving with the Potential-Based Approach means choosing to serve what is emerging as the greatest potential of the moment rather than serving the problem. We go straight to potential, ask the potential to show us possibilities that could serve that potential, choose the possibility that speaks to us the most, and let the energy of the potential and possibility show us the way to creation and new outcome.

In the context of the Four Levels of Engagement, the Potential-Based Approach takes us directly to Choice and Opportunity. In the context of the vertical and horizontal planes of awareness, it takes us into the vertical, where we can step out of the three-dimensional reality for a time and perceive a much bigger picture. From there we can partner and cocreate with the potential waiting to emerge, ultimately making a difference in the horizontal plane.

The Potential-Based Approach in Action

Implementing the Potential-Based Approach takes five simple steps:

1. Expand Awareness. Make sure you are in an expanded state of awareness. You can use the Point of Stillness technique or any of the other intuitive tools introduced in previous chapters to help you step beyond the intellectual mind into the intuitive.

2. Perceive Potential. Ask, "What is the greatest potential wanting to emerge? What is really wanting to happen here?"

3. Create a Reality Field. Creating a reality field is about becoming a human embodiment of the potential that is waiting to unfold and creating an energetic field that vibrates to the frequency of the potential. The Principle of Attraction states that vibrations of like frequency will attract one another. Therefore, we must embody the potential; we must shift our vibrational frequency to match that of the potential. In this way, we create a field of energy that vibrates to the frequency of the new reality we wish to create, greatly increasing the chances that the potential will manifest in form. You will learn much more about reality fields in the next few chapters.

4. Commit Once and for All. Ask the potential what the breakthrough is for you and the situation, and what once-and-for-all commitment it is calling for. Recognize what permanent shift must occur in your thought, belief, attitudes, behavior, and/or practices in order for you to live in this new vibrational frequency. And then make the commitment once and for all.

5. Follow the Energy. Surrender to the potential, consider the possible ways that potential could manifest in form, choose the possibility you feel called to, and let it show you the way to its creation. As you stand in the energy of that potential and possibility, what actions or steps are you now called to take? What wants to happen or be accomplished within the next six months? In the next month? In the next week? Today?

The Potential-Based Approach is a powerful model. It is a vehicle for transformation. Sometimes you will follow the model through its five steps. Other times you will employ only the steps that are appropriate for the moment. Let the Potential-Based Approach be a way of thinking or a new paradigm from which you and those you serve operate rather than a fixed formula, and it will serve you well.

Inquiry: The Potential-Based Approach vs. the Problem-Solving Approach

Bring to mind a personal or professional situation that you have been approaching as a problem to be solved. Then consider what could happen if you approached it as potential waiting to unfold.

➤ What is the potential?
➤ What are the possibilities—the possible ways that the potential could manifest? Which possibility do you choose to partner with?
➤ What breakthrough could allow that potential and possibility to unfold?
➤ What next steps are the breakthrough and potential asking you to take?

PROBLEM-SOLVING APPROACH VS. POTENTIAL-BASED APPROACH

	PROBLEM-SOLVING APPROACH	POTENTIAL-BASED APPROACH
OPERATIVE INTELLIGENCE	Primarily based in problem-solving and a physical, rational, intellectual approach.	Expansive, intuitive, and soul-connected while incorporating rational intellect; based in creating new realities rather than solving problems.
STARTING POINT FOR DECISIONS AND THE EXPLORATION OF POSSIBILITIES	Current reality and/or the past—how to make what is better or avoid what was.	Future, potential-based approach, breaking free from current contexts. "Let the potential lead the way."
UNDERSTANDING OF HOW THE WORLD WORKS	Classical-physics principles: the three-dimensional world is what we know; learning the rules of the physical world leads to knowledge, wisdom, and success.	Quantum-physics principles: multiple dimensions exist simultaneously; learning rules of physical world and quantum world leads to knowledge, wisdom, and success.
UNDERSTANDING OF TIME	Time is linear and fixed. Cause and effect require direct contact or relationships.	Time is linear, circular, or simultaneous; past, present, and future can coexist; direct physical or verbal contact isn't required for people, events, or objects to influence one another.
MANIFESTATION PROCESS	Generally focused on making things happen. "How hard will I have to push to achieve results?"	Focus is on potential and harnessing the inherent power of people, organizations, and situations. "What wants to happen here, and how can I partner with what is emerging?"
CHANGE PROCESS	Linear and dependent on a sequence of events that move through linear time.	Instantaneous when the right conditions are present.

➤ How does your situation feel different when you approach it as potential waiting to unfold rather than a problem to be solved?

➤ How might the process and experience of leadership or service change for both you and those you serve if you employed the Potential-Based Approach rather than a problem-solving approach?

CHAPTER EIGHTEEN

The Nature of Reality Fields

The feelings that result from your life experience, your joy, pain and all variations of these extremes are, quite literally, teaching you how to think and feel frequency. Your thoughts are the tool that you use to bring yourself into resonance with various aspects of creation. Thoughts and feelings are your tuning mechanisms. When the tuning is optimum, you have established resonance, a connection of two-way exchange with a given level of reality.
—GREGG BRADEN, *author of* Awakening to Zero Point

When our awareness is limited to the three-dimensional world and the laws of classical physics, it is easy to get caught in the assumption that our current interpretation of reality is all there is. We think that our only option is to work with the present circumstance and try to make it better or change it over time. Even if we know on some level that there are other possibilities, we easily forget that truth because the mass consciousness is conditioned to operate from Drama and Situation rather than Choice and Opportunity.

Throughout this book, however, we've been acknowledging that there are actually many options. Step by step, we've been expanding beyond three-dimensional awareness into quantum awareness. In these next three chapters, we will explore reality fields and how they can speed up the transformation and creative process, especially when employed as a part of the Potential-Based Approach.

We recognize the quantum field as the field of pure potential, created and sustained by Consciousness. As explained in chapter 15, we live in an open universe, meaning that everything is made up of energy in motion and with no preset form. At the quantum level, we, our circumstances, and our organizations are also open—energy in motion and with no preset form. It is at the quantum level that we can become active participants in the cocreation of our present and future. Energy is where we must keep our focus, because when we work at the level of energetic essence, we are in that open space where anything is possible.

Chapter 12 spoke of quantum leaps. When something makes a quantum leap, it jumps, whole and complete, from one place to another. There is no transition phase, no process of change; it simply disappears from one place and simultaneously reappears in another.

The technology of reality fields shows us *how* to make quantum shifts in thoughts, attitudes, perspectives, beliefs, and senses of being. When we make these quantum shifts, who we are within our circumstance changes, as does our relationship to the circumstance. We become aware of possibilities and potential that we had not been able to perceive before.

Wave-particle theory shows us that waves of possibility have no specific form or space-time location until they are observed. The quantum field contains many waves of possibilities. At the point of observation, they collapse into particles, which can be measured within a local space and time. This phenomenon leads us to the notion that through observation, we create reality. As soon as we observe the wave pattern, it collapses into a particle and then exists in form in a specific space-time location. Therefore, how we choose to observe and engage our circumstance determines our relationship to it and the particular reality we inhabit.

The Potential-Based Approach is all about working with waves of potential in the open space, about engaging and communicating with the quantum field. Creation and manifestation then become, metaphorically speaking, an energetic conversation within the quantum field—energy communicating with energy, one vibrational frequency communicating with another.

We communicate energetically with the quantum field and

Consciousness through our vibrational frequency. The vibrational frequency that we project into our environment creates a field of energy that I call a reality field. A reality field is a physical or non-physical space that vibrates to a particular frequency. That particular frequency will determine the conditions, experiences, opportunities, challenges, and synchronicities that are drawn into or occur in connection with that reality field. In other words, the reality is significantly influenced by the vibrational frequency of the energetic field. Reality fields are a fact of life. They exist everywhere. We can choose to live in the reality fields created by circumstances and other people, or we can be proactive and intentionally create reality fields that will serve who we are called to be and what we are called to do.

Remember the eight-sided mirror metaphor for the holographic principle. That metaphor illustrates how you are the center and cause of the reality field you create for yourself. To be more specific, your thoughts, beliefs, and actions create your personal holographic universe—your reality field. We are all constantly creating our own holographic universes—our own reality fields—whether or not we are aware of doing so.

In the Potential-Based Approach, we partner with potential, which means that we embody the energy of the potential that is waiting to unfold. We match our own vibrational frequency to that of the potential. In essence, we become it. We are no longer separate from it and observing it or working with it. "Observing it" or "working with it" imply that we and the potential are separate. "Embodying it" means that we *are* it. By vibrating at the same frequency as the potential, we become one with it at an energetic level.

When we become the energy of the potential, we create a new reality field simply through our being. Because this reality field vibrates to the same frequency as the potential, it will start to attract the optimal conditions necessary for the potential to manifest in form. Here are the hermetic Principles of Vibration and Attraction at work. As a result of the reality field, things start to happen. Our *response* to the things that happen is our action of being—the next obvious step as the energy leads the way.

We cannot exist or function independently of the space and objects around us. Who we are and what we do are recognized and defined by the impact we have physically and energetically on our environment. Everything exists in a field of energy that is created and influenced by the vibrational frequency of the person, object, or idea that is at its center. The more powerful the focus, intensity, and commitment of the person, object, or idea, the stronger, more dynamic, and more powerful the field will be, and the greater its influence on anything that enters into that field will be. The stronger vibrational frequency will prevail.

Energy does not recognize human organizational structures or who holds the title of boss, supervisor, or leader. It recognizes only focus and vibrational intensity and frequency. This concept is important to transformational work. The person, group, belief, or idea that is the most focused and has the greatest intensity of vibration holds the energetic power in any situation and will be the driving force. At any particular time, the energetic leadership may be coming from the top of an organization, or it may be coming from the bottom or the middle. It may even be coming from a cultural belief that most of the people in the group are subscribing to.

An important skill in transformational work is being able to recognize where the energetic power or driving force is at all times. Are you and/or your philosophy or vision that driving force, or is someone or something else? If things are moving in the direction you understand to be the greatest potential, then let the driving force continue. If not, what needs to shift within you or your organization in order to focus the energy, raise the vibrational frequency, and increase its intensity? What needs to shift so that the energetic driving force of the situation is once again carrying you toward the greatest potential?

All possibilities for the future are present in the waves of the quantum field. When you create reality fields, you are actually creating the energetic conditions that will attract the future outcome you feel called to create. You are setting up the conditions that will encourage the wave to collapse into a particular particle. Your individual choices and the reality field you create determine which of the possibilities you are likely to experience.

It is very important to note that when you create a reality field, *you are not creating a specific reality; you are creating a field of energy that vibrates at a particular frequency.* In partnering with potential, you are creating a reality field that vibrates at the same frequency as the emerging potential. Remember the Principle of Attraction: like attracts like. Whatever reality field you allow or create will attract outcomes and circumstances that match its vibrational frequency.

When you fully embody the energy of that which you wish to create, the holographic principle is activated and reflects the energy matrix of that new reality out into the world. In that moment, you have created a new reality field. By creating reality fields, you actively partner with the quantum field and Consciousness for cocreation.

When you work from the quantum level, there are an infinite number of reality fields available to you at any one time. Imagine a multilane highway in which each lane ultimately leads to a different destination. Each lane represents a different reality field. You choose which lane to travel in. That choice is determined by your thoughts and beliefs. The traffic in each lane moves at a different speed and vibrational frequency. You have an effect on the lane by choosing it; at the same time, the lane you choose influences who you are, your relationships to those around you, your thoughts, and your beliefs. If you say that you want a different destination, but do not change lanes by changing your thoughts, beliefs, and choices, then you will not reach the destination or outcome you say that you want. Instead, you will live in the reality field that is created and supported by your thoughts, beliefs, and actions.

The once-and-for-all commitment that is part of the Potential-Based Approach is a permanent lane change. We all have our default or habitual thoughts, beliefs, and choices. They determine which lane of the highway we travel in—which reality field we create—whether or not we are aware of them. If we wish to change lanes, we must make a once-and-for-all commitment to shifting our thoughts, beliefs, and actions. And then we must continue to reinforce that commitment until it becomes our new default lane. Otherwise, the lane shift will be temporary, and we will soon find ourselves traveling in our old default lane once again. In other words, for the transformation to be sustainable, we must consciously and repeatedly choose the reality field we wish to live in. We have the power to choose who we are and what we think, believe, and do; we have the power to choose what is at the center of our personal reality field.

As more and more people make similar choices or hold the same beliefs, the holographic patterning in our culture becomes stronger. Enough people must sustain the same reality field at the same time in order for systemic change to occur. When they do, we reach the critical mass required for sustainable change in the mass consciousness.

Inquiry: Energy and Power

➤ What are the strongest energy forces in your life? In what ways are they serving you, supporting your efforts to reach your greatest potential? How are they getting in your way? What insights arise from this inquiry?

➤ Think about groups that you are a part of, either in your work or in your personal life. Who or what holds the energetic power in those groups? Look for examples of official leaders holding the power as well as examples of true power coming from some one who is not the official leader. What insights do you gain from these observations?

➤ What evidence do you have of thoughts, emotions, and actions creating reality fields? What is the reality field that you live in most of the time?

➤ How could you apply the concepts of reality fields in your leadership and service?

CHAPTER NINETEEN

Creating Intentional Reality Fields

When you are inspired by some great purpose, some extraordinary project, all your thoughts break their bonds: Your mind transcends limitations, your consciousness expands in every direction, and you find yourself in a new, great and wonderful world. Dormant forces, faculties and talents become alive, and you discover yourself to be a greater person by far than you ever dreamed yourself to be.

—PATAÑJALI, *father of yoga*

Now that you understand what reality fields are and why awareness of them is important, let's look more deeply into their anatomy and how we can consciously create fields that support transformational work.

Chapter 9 talked about the three intelligences within us: Thought, Emotion, and Truth. Thought dwells in the head and is our intellectual ability to comprehend information, make a plan, and implement it. Emotion dwells in the lower body and is our passion and fuel, as well as our fundamental beliefs about whatever issue we might be addressing. Truth dwells in the heart and offers a more expanded awareness about our situation.

These intelligences offer insight into why we feel the way we do and why we make the choices and decisions we make. Together, these three intelligences and the alignment between them create their own reality field.

Thought + Emotion + Truth ➞ Reality Field

Moreover, all three intelligences must be engaged for that power-ful intentional reality field to exist. If any one of them is missing, the reality field will be weak or not support what you want to cre-ate. When you have Emotion without Thought, you experience great passion and power for making something happen, but lack direction and focus. You can't seem to formulate a plan. On the other hand, when you have Thought without Emotion, you may experience clear direction and focus and be able to make a great plan, but there is no passion or excitement behind that direction and focus. Thought has very little energy or fuel without a wave of Emotion. As soon as you attach Thought to a wave of Emotion (which is energy), that Thought has power.

The heart holds your greater Truth. Through your heart, you are able to see a big-picture view. If you are not able to get in touch with the Truth of your heart, you will lack a sense of a big picture, even if Thought and Emotion are present.

Not only must all three intelligences be engaged, but they must also be in alignment with one another. When they are aligned, the result is a potent reality field. That reality field will attract condi-tions and outcomes of similar vibrational frequency. When Thought, Emotion, and Truth are not in alignment, the resulting reality field is chaotic, weak, or confused, again attracting similar circumstances and conditions.

The ancient wisdom traditions teach us that there are two funda-mental emotions: love and fear. All other emotions are rooted in one or the other. Whether the present Emotion intelligence is rooted in love or fear is another significant factor in the resulting vibrational frequency of the reality field. If the Emotion is love, then Thought and Truth are fueled with positive energy and excitement. This com-bination creates a reality field of empowerment and authentic con-fidence that will vibrate at a higher frequency and likely attract the outcomes you desire. If, on the other hand, the Emotion is fear, then

Thought = focus
direction
guidance

Truth = greater intuitive knowing

Emotion = passion
fuel
belief

Thought + Emotion + Truth → Reality Field

Thought and Truth are fueled with doubt, resistance, misgivings, and other emotions that hold you back, keep you trapped, or cause you to act purely in reaction to those feelings. The resulting reality field is then grounded in fear and vibrates at a lower frequency. It will attract what you most fear or resist. Therefore, it is imperative for you to be aware of the fundamental Emotion feeding your reality field.

Exploration: Creating a Reality Field by Identifying and Aligning Emotion, Thought, and Truth

Bring to your awareness a vision, project, or goal, either from your personal life or related to your work. What wants to happen through that vision or project? What is the potential waiting to unfold?

Once you have identified the potential, begin by focusing your attention on your Thought. What do you think about this potential? What is the story you tell yourself about it? What does your intellect tell you? Make no judgment about what you discover. Just observe. What are your thoughts?

Now drop down into your body and focus all of your awareness on what Emotion has to say about the potential and this project. What emotions do you experience when you focus your attention on this potential? What story does Emotion tell you about it? Just observe. Is your Emotion based in love or fear? Again, make no judgment on what you discover. You don't have to do anything about what you observe. Just notice.

Now go to your heart center. What is your Truth about this project or vision and its potential? What do you know in your heart?

Breathe into the overall energy being created by Thought, Emotion, and Truth. This energy is your current reality field for this vision or project. That reality field is now being reflected out through the holographic universe. How would you describe the reality field that is being created right now? Are Thought, Emotion, and Truth in alignment with one another? Does this reality field serve you and support your project?

If so, continue to breathe into that reality field, reinforcing the energy so that it can continue to strengthen and sustain your project.

If not, let's discover what needs to shift in order for these three components to be brought into alignment with one another and create a reality field that will best support you. Begin by dropping back down into Emotion. Is the fundamental Emotion love or fear? If it is fear, choose love instead. Don't fret over how to do it. Just intend it—choose love—and notice how the reality field starts to shift.

Then, while staying anchored in the Emotion of love, go back to your Thought, to your head. What are your thoughts telling you now? They may have already shifted somewhat when you chose love as your fundamental Emotion. Whatever your thoughts are, do they serve you? Again, make no judgment; just observe. If your thoughts are not serving you, be curious and listen to their concern, the story your Thought is telling. Does that story belong to the present moment or to another time? Is that story true today? If it is true, what is the story asking you to reconsider about your project? If it is not true today, what story do you choose now?

In most cases, if the Emotion is love and Truth tells you that this is the right path, then the resistance coming from your thoughts is actually no longer relevant, nor is the story that goes with that resistance. They belong to another time—a time when that resistance and story may have served you well—but they do not apply to today. So the question becomes, how do you choose to think about this project and its potential now?

Finally, return to the heart. What is your Truth now? If anything is unsettled here, take time to explore that feeling. Be curious. Does some aspect of the project need to be reconsidered, or does the Truth feel uncomfortable because it is asking you to stretch or make a breakthrough? Either one could be the case. Pay attention and be honest with yourself.

Having done your work in the heart, bring your awareness back to all three intelligences. Are they in alignment now? Do they create a reality field that serves you? If so, continue to reinforce this reality field. If not, continue your dialogue with Thought, Emotion, and Truth, being curious and compassionate, as well as diligent, until you reach a reality field that will carry you forward to the greatest potential.

Reality fields are part of the technology of creation and transforma-tion. Transformational Presence is ultimately the result of a pow-erfully aligned and focused reality field. Reality fields are an inner technology of awareness, discipline, and action. For the technology to work, you must have a clear focus and intention (Thought) on what the new reality is and an ability to listen to the new reality and take direction from it. The fundamental Emotion must be love. In addi-tion, you must have great passion for the new reality and an absolute belief that the new reality is possible. The Truth of the heart must tell you that this is the right path. The powerful reality field created from this alignment initiates an energy conversation with the quan-tum field and projects a holographic image. As a result, a new reality in the three-dimensional world begins to take form.

Just as your Thought, Emotion, and Truth are constantly re-creating or reinforcing your reality field, your current reality field, regardless of whether or not you are aware of it, is constantly re-creating or reinforcing your Thought, Emotion, and Truth. To the degree that you let them, outside influences constantly affect you as well. This leads to an ongoing cycle:

Thought + Emotion + Truth → Reality Field → Thought
+ Emotion + Truth → Reality Field (and so on)

You are fully responsible for the reality field in which you live. If you allow someone or something else to create your reality field, you have given away your power to create your own reality. You must be honest about the source of your current reality field before you can create a different one.

Coming up against reality fields created by daily experiences is a part of life in the horizontal world. From time to time, another real-ity field may take you by surprise and throw you off balance. When it does, pause, take a deep breath, acknowledge what is going on around you and inside you, choose the alternate reality field that will serve you in the moment, and work through your Thought, Emotion, and Truth to reinforce and sustain it.

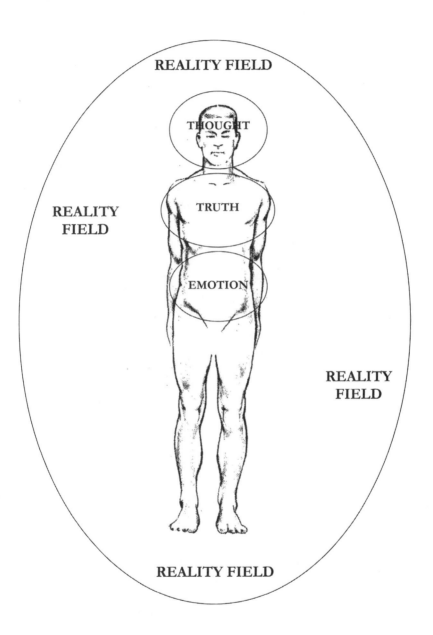

When you first create a new reality field, it will not yet be your habitual way of living. You must vigilantly reinforce the new field until it becomes your default. The new reality field will then guide you through each choice, decision, or action. Again, the most effective action comes out of being. Embody the new reality, and it will begin to show you the steps to take.

Your reality field goes with you wherever you go. Everyone who steps into your reality field will be affected by it. Therefore, awareness of and great skill in working with reality fields is essential for anyone wishing to have Transformational Presence. Remember that the stronger vibrational frequency will prevail in any situation. When you experience a challenging reality field of another person or situation, you can counter that energy by increasing the intensity of your Thought, Emotion, and Truth, thereby strengthening the vibrational frequency of your own reality field. This is much more effective and efficient than stepping into an offensive or defensive position against that person or situation, or fending off their reality field. Becoming defensive or offensive actually gives energy to their position. Instead, you are sustaining and strengthening *your* reality field and taking actions accordingly.

In transformational leadership and service, part of our job is to help those we serve create and maintain powerful and sustainable reality fields. We help them become aware of the impact of those fields and whether or not the effects are in alignment and harmony with their essence—their souls—and with the greatest potential that is showing itself. We support their effort to live and work guided by soul and what wants to happen in the big picture.

As we serve others, we must continue to be aware that our own Thought, Emotion, and Truth are creating our personal reality fields in every moment. Which lane of the highway are we traveling in? What is the reality field we are creating? And will our current reality field support and sustain the greater potential that is wanting to unfold?

The following Exploration is a variation on the future-self Exploration from chapter 8 and incorporates the Potential-Based Approach. It can help you tap into potential and invite that potential to create the reality field that will best serve its realization.

Exploration: Creating a Reality Field from Your Vision or Project Potential

Stand with enough space in front of you to take a couple of steps forward. Close your eyes and take a moment to find your inner Point of Stillness. Bring to mind your vision or project from the last exercise and ask, "What is the greatest potential for this vision or project?"

As that potential becomes clear, imagine that standing in front of you is a future version of yourself, one who has completed the project and realized its potential. Look into your future self's eyes. Feel his or her energy. Let your awareness take you beyond the form standing in front of you to the underlying energy. As you look directly into the eyes of this future version of you, feel those eyes looking directly into you. How would you describe this version of you? What are his or her energetic qualities?

Ask your future self how he or she got to be there, fully living this potential. Ask what steps or path led to where he or she is now. Ask what advice this future self has for you.

When you are ready, while still looking directly into your future self's eyes, literally step forward and trade places with that self. Step into his or her energy. Become your future self.

Notice how your energy shifts. How has your reality field shifted? How do you feel different? Check your Emotion; what is it? What are your thoughts? What is the Truth in your heart? Note how the three intelligences are aligned now that the potential is fully realized. What new insight or understanding do you have about your project or vision?

What is the opportunity available here for a personal breakthrough or shift? Claim that breakthrough once and for all.

As you stand in the energy of the fully realized potential, what actions or steps are you called to take? What wants to happen or be accomplished within the next six months?

Zooming in now, what must be your focus over the next month?

Zooming in even more, what needs to be your focus for the next week?

And finally, what needs to be your focus for the rest of today?

Follow the instructions or guidance you have just received. Step into action of being and continue listening to the potential as it shows you the way forward.

CHAPTER TWENTY

Keeping the Intentional Reality Field Alive and Vibrant

A man sooner or later discovers that he is the master-gardener
of his soul, the director of his life.

—JAMES ALLEN, *philosopher and poet*

Once you have intentionally created a reality field and are sustaining it, the energy may still slip from time to time. Or things may not seem to be going as well as you think they could. These are signs that something is not in alignment, that there is an energy leak in the system.

Imagine a garden hose attached to a water source that provides good, strong, steady water pressure. Then imagine that a tiny hole develops in the hose. As water leaks through the small hole, the water pressure through the hose drops slightly. Over time, the water leak makes the hole bigger, and the water pressure drops even more. The tiny leak becomes more and more powerful because it is robbing the hose of its full potential to water the garden.

Energy leaks do to a reality field what such water leaks do to a garden hose. When the reality field is intact and sustained by the complete alignment of your Thought, Emotion, and Truth, amazing things happen. However, if there is just one tiny doubt, fear, or resistance—any part of your Thought, Emotion, or Truth that is not in complete alignment with your new reality field—there is a leak in the hose. A leak anywhere in the reality field drains energy and makes the reality field less potent. Ninety-nine percent of your Thought, Emotion, and Truth may be supporting the vibrational frequency of the new reality field, but the 1 percent that isn't can keep you from realizing the potential. There are several possible causes for energy leaks. The first place to look is Thought, Emotion, and Truth; make sure they are all fully engaged. If any one is missing, there is not enough energy to support a strong reality field. If all are engaged, then check whether or not the three intelligences are in alignment with one another. Are they perhaps creating a reality field that is working against the potential instead of supporting it?

Energy leaks can also be caused by hidden agendas—a desire or goal that is not openly expressed. In an individual, a hidden agenda may show up as an unconscious and/or unacknowledged fear or desire that has its own motivation for making sure that you do not succeed. In a group or organization, hidden agendas occur when one or more members of the group have conflicting ideas about what should be happening or personal motivations that are not in alignment with the group's stated goals. Those holding these conflicting ideas and personal motivations are often not fully open and transparent about their intentions.

Adopting someone else's reality field or the reality field of an idea or principle that is not in harmony with who you are at your essence can also cause an energy leak. An example might be trying to adopt the reality field of your company or organization when what that company stands for is in conflict with your fundamental values. Leaks also occur when you allow your current circumstance to be the prevailing reality field instead of the underlying potential.

Taking some time for the following exercise will help you learn how to scan for energy leaks, repair them, and return to a potent reality field.

Exploration: Scanning for Leaks

This exercise is best done in an open indoor or outdoor space where you can move around. Begin by taking a few moments to be sure you are in a state of expanded awareness. Then stand in a spot you choose to represent this present time.

Choose a project or goal you are currently working on. Take time to tap into the potential that is waiting to unfold. Then focus your attention on your Thought. What are your thoughts about this project and its potential? Just observe. Don't get caught up in them or make any judgment about them. You are simply gathering information. At this point, you don't need to shift or fix anything. Just notice if anything in your Thought is getting in your way of realizing this potential.

Once you have identified your thoughts, drop down into your lower body and focus your awareness solely on your Emotion. What are your beliefs about this project and its potential? Do you believe it can happen? What is your level of passion for it? What do you experience as Emotion? Is the Emotion fundamentally love or fear? Again, make no judgment. Just observe. You don't need to fix or shift anything. Just take note of any resistance or fear that is getting in your way.

Now move to your heart. What is the Truth there? What is your greater knowing about this project and its potential?

What is the resulting reality field? How would you describe it? Just observe this reality field, allowing it to be whatever it is.

Now move to stand in a different spot, which can represent a year after this project or goal has been accomplished and its potential fully realized. Feel the energy there and embody it. Pay attention to the qualities of the energy. What is the reality field? How does it feel?

While standing in this new reality field, once again focus your awareness solely on your Thought. What are your thoughts a year after the project has been completed?

Then shift your focus to your Emotion. What do you experience?

Shift your awareness to your heart center. What is your Truth?

Become aware of the reality field being created by Thought, Emotion, and Truth together as you stand in the place where the project is complete and the potential realized. Breathe deeply into this reality field so that you fully embody it. Then, remaining firmly grounded in this reality field and in this Thought, Emotion, and Truth, go back to the spot that represents the present, *bringing the reality field of the future with you.*

Take a moment to locate yourself back in the present and let the reality field of the future become your present-moment reality field.

As you stand in the new reality field, explore your Thought once again. What has shifted? Are there any thoughts that are still getting in the way of you reaching that future? Just observe.

Continuing to stand in the new reality field, focus on your Emotion. How has it shifted? Is anything in your Emotion still getting in the way of you reaching the full potential? Again, just observe.

Then go to your heart. What is your Truth now? Is anything in this Truth standing in the way of your forward movement?

How would you describe this new reality field? Is it as potent as it was in the future? If so, continue to reinforce the Thought, Emotion, and Truth creating this field.

If you still perceive blocks in Thought, Emotion, or Truth, go back to the future spot again, where the project has been completed and you've been living in that potential for a year. In that reality, you clearly had gotten past those blocks. What does this future reality field tell you about them?

Once the blocks are resolved, return to the spot representing the present moment, *taking the future reality field with you* once again.

Take time to check in with Thought, Emotion, and Truth once more. Continue this process of dialogue and resolution between the future and the present until you are able to hold the reality field of the future in the present time. And then memorize that feeling.

What is now clear to you about completing your project and realizing its potential? What are your next steps? What wants to happen or be accomplished in the next six months? The next month? The next week? Today?

When you discover a leak, it is easy to judge that leak to be a bad thing. However, leaks are often symptoms of a larger issue—a fear, a doubt, a disbelief, or a disharmony that needs to be addressed. Therefore, leaks are often important messages. They can help you find the proper alignment that makes the realization of goals and visions possible. Engage the leak in dialogue. Be curious and compassionate. Discover what caused that leak—what message is trying to get through. And then respond.

Scanning for Leaks: Simple Steps

1. Stand in a spot that represents the present moment. Identify your current Emotion, Thought, Truth, and the resulting reality field.
2. Move to a spot that will represent a year after the potential has been fully realized. Identify your Emotion, Thought, Truth, and the resulting reality field.
3. Return to the spot representing the present moment, *bringing with you the reality field of the future.* Explore Emotion, Thought, and Truth once again. How have they changed?
4. If there are lingering doubts, fears, or resistance, take them back to the future and address them from the future reality field.
5. Return to the present-moment spot and claim this future reality field for the present. What do you now know about your next steps?

It is important to check in periodically and take stock of the energy status of the reality field and how things are developing. You must tend your reality fields just as you would tend a garden. Weeds must be pulled, and the garden must be watered. In reality fields, leaks must be fixed, and the energy must be sustained. From time to time, pause to ask, "Is this reality field serving me and the greatest potential in the best possible way?"

If you find that your current reality field is not serving you, go back to the Scanning for Leaks Exploration to identify and repair leaks. You can also go back to the reality field formula—Thought + Emotion + Truth ➜ Reality Field—and work backwards through it. Start by imagining the reality field that would serve you. What Truth would support that reality field? Imagine that Truth. What Thought and Emotion would support that field? Imagine them and embody them now. What reality field are you now creating?

Inquiry: Powerful Questions for Scanning for Leaks

When you are scanning for energy leaks, powerful questions can quickly move the process forward and cut to the heart of the matter. Powerful questions are open questions that take us and those we serve deeper in our awareness. Closed questions, by contrast, demand a yes-or-no answer and, therefore, do not necessarily take us to another level.

Here are some examples of powerful questions. What other questions would you add to the list?

- ➤ What is your soul's truth here?
- ➤ What do you absolutely know from here?
- ➤ What do you fear from here?
- ➤ What do you resist about this?
- ➤ Who would you be without that fear or resistance?
- ➤ What does your soul say or know about that fear and resistance?
- ➤ What is the gift of this setback, fear, or resistance? What does it want you to see, hear, or be aware of?
- ➤ Who are *you* in that picture?
- ➤ Who do you choose to be in this situation?
- ➤ What do you choose to do with that information?
- ➤ What are at least three possibilities here?
- ➤ What story are you telling yourself right now? Is the story serving you? Do you choose to stick with your story or change it? What difference does your choice make?
- ➤ What is one shift that would make everything different?

The principles of individual reality fields can also apply to group reality fields. Group reality fields are made up of the Thought, Emotion, and Truth that dominate the group. Scanning for leaks within a group means exploring the Thought, Emotion, and Truth the overall group has about the vision, project, or goal. That process will usually require some work at the individual level. Each member of the group or team must create their own powerful reality fields for the project and repair energy leaks in those fields. Creating and repairing individual group members' fields, in turn, will create a powerful and dynamic group reality field. Once that new reality field is in place, nurtured, and sustained, things can move forward in greater ease and flow, and your group stands a very good chance of surpassing its goals.

I am sometimes asked how reality-field creation is different from traditional prayer. Prayer, as it is most often practiced in mainstream Western culture, is essentially a request to God for something to happen. When you ask for something to happen, you are, in effect, reinforcing the fact that it has not yet happened. You reinforce the separation between you and what you desire. Prayer in this form can actually be *dis*empowering if you are simply asking for something to be taken care of without claiming your personal power, role, or responsibility in its creation or manifestation.

Creating reality fields, on the other hand, involves fully claiming your role in the active creation of the new circumstance. You shift your vibrational frequency to a new level. You step into powerful cocreation with Consciousness instead of waiting for an outside force—God, Consciousness, or someone or something else—to take care of it.

Transformational Presence is not so much about words or philosophies, or even about action. At its essence, it is about embodying vibrational frequencies. Your vibrational frequency determines your state of being, which then informs and creates your presence, words, and actions. To effect change in our lives and in the world—indeed to create a world that works—we must embody the new conditions, the potential wanting to unfold. The Principle of Correspondence and the holographic principle will then reflect that vibrational frequency out into the world. That vibrational frequency will also inform your action. You will intuitively know the next steps to be taken and how to take those steps.

Embodiment of the energy is the key. Otherwise, you and whatever you wish to manifest remain separate, and your reality field continues to vibrate to the frequency of your current circumstance rather than to the frequency of what you want to manifest.

Creating a world that works begins with creating *within ourselves* the conditions that we are called to create in our world. When we create a reality field through our full embodiment of the energy, that field is reflected outward. Mastery of reality-field technology builds a powerful faith that says what you are called to create will indeed happen. Faith is belief that does not depend on logical proof or material evidence. Faith is not a function of Thought, Emotion, or Truth alone, but a function of all three in alignment. In reality-field technology, having faith means that you have fully accepted and embraced your power as a directive force in the creation of a new reality. You have partnered with potential and Consciousness, and you are working through the quantum field. You are empowered to do your part to help our world reach its greatest potential as a global civilization. A reality field is not a substitute for an action plan. It is a consciousness that you embody. However, through employing the Potential-Based Approach, an action plan will emerge from the energy of the reality field as you follow the guidance and inspiration of the potential. Through your expanded awareness and the new intuitive knowledge gained through these approaches, the action plan begins to take shape. Most importantly, it is a plan that is grounded in the energetic essence of the potential. Your action plan then becomes potential creating form. *You* become Consciousness in creation.

Transformational Presence means creating the conditions for new realities to manifest. It demands that we become skilled at creating reality fields by doing the appropriate work with our Thought, Emotion, and Truth. In turn, we help those we serve become skilled in this area. Transformation and change, whether within individuals or in organizations, can happen very quickly—like quantum leaps—when we master reality-field technology. Imagine how mastering that technology could impact our world. In fact, create that reality field right now and see what happens.

Inquiry: Reality Fields and Transformational Presence
➤ How do this chapter and all this book has talked about help you more fully understand and explain life as energy in motion?
➤ What would shift in your life if you fully embraced your power as a directive force in the creation of a new reality?
➤ Are the action plans in your life and work informed by reality fields, or are reality fields informed by your action plans? In what areas of your life or work can you apply the Potential-Based Approach to create an action plan? What difference could that make?
➤ What are some examples of group reality fields that you have observed? What realities were created from those fields?

FROM VERTICAL TO HORIZONTAL: TRANSFORMATIONAL PRESENCE IN ACTION

CHAPTER TWENTY-ONE

Praxis and Practice: Closing the Gap Between Knowledge and Action

In its essence, leadership is about learning how to shape the future. Leadership exists when people are no longer victims of circumstances but participate in creating new circumstances. . . . Leadership is about creating a domain in which human beings continually deepen their understanding of reality and become more capable of participating in the unfolding of the world. Ultimately, leadership is about creating new realities.

—PETER SENGE, *founding chair, Society for Organizational Learning*

Many of us are fairly sophisticated in our knowledge. We know a lot, whether that knowledge has been gleaned from formal study, life experience, teachers and mentors, intuitive assimilation, or all of the above. However, we don't always live what we know. For most of us, there remain gaps between what we know and how we live, between what is and what could be, between what is available to us and what we actually access. There may be a hurdle we must clear or a breakthrough we must make. Chapter 17 spoke of closing the gaps by introducing the four fundamental principles of the Potential-Based Approach. In this chapter, we go deeper into what closing the gaps means within the context of Transformational Presence and creating a world that works.

Closing the gap involves periodically assessing where you are, asking questions such as: Do I live what I know? Are my life and work truly informed by my knowledge? Do I apply what I know on a daily basis? Are these concepts becoming a natural part of my ongoing life? Am I developing the wisdom to use my knowledge most effectively?

Closing the gap involves practice and praxis. In chapter 17, praxis was defined as the integration of belief with behavior. It's how you bring it all together. Praxis is closing the gap. Practice, in this context, is how you get there—the path and discipline required to achieve praxis. The root of *discipline* is *disciple.* Praxis invites you to consider what you are called to be a disciple to—what you are being called to live fully and completely with every breath, word, and action. Praxis calls forth the greatness of the human spirit.

Praxis means not only *knowing* your essence and truth, but also *living* it through your choices and actions. Having a skill and not using it is the same as not having it. Having a belief but not honoring it is the same as not believing. Your life can give to you only what you give to it. If you don't plant seeds, there is no harvest. If you don't lead from your truth, you don't get results that are in harmony with your truth. Be totally honest about the thoughts, intentions, beliefs, and actions that you choose. Will they lead to the realization of your greatest potential? Close the gap between what you know and how you live.

Praxis is the practical application of Shakespeare's famous phrase "to thine own self be true." Even though you may have done a tremendous amount of inner work, stepping into action—even action inspired by and rooted in Transformational Presence—can still uncover deeply buried, unresolved inner conflicts. We are conditioned by society to fit into the crowd, to play it safe, to not call attention to ourselves. When we commit to living our greatest potential, we may hear conflicted inner messages like, "Be as good as you can, but know your limitations. Don't get too full of yourself," or "Don't set your sights too high. People in our family don't get those kinds of jobs/don't have that kind of success/don't get ahead in life." Or an inner voice might scream, "Who do you think you are?"

There are generations of thoughts and beliefs programmed into every cell of your being. Sometimes they serve you; sometimes they get in your way. Those thoughts and beliefs can shape every step of your journey if you let them. Your power to choose, however, can override your preexisting conditioning. Making the choice to follow your own path, to honor your personal truth, to focus on potential rather than circumstance, to practice praxis may not be comfortable, but you *can* do these things, and they are essential to your success.

Transformational Presence requires praxis—integrating your know-ledge with your behavior, bringing together what you *know* needs to be done with *actually doing it.* Praxis often means working through deeply ingrained personal fears so that you are able to accomplish your present goals. It's not always as simple as deciding you are going to think or believe differently and then just doing it. To experience complete peace and harmony with a thought or belief, you must work through whatever issues arise in response to the desired shift. These issues may have stories that have not yet been resolved. You must listen to that part of you holding on tightly to a thought or belief to find out what assurance it needs from you. How can you provide that assurance? It is ultimately up to you to heal those parts of yourself, transforming your fears and doubts into courage and confidence. I don't know any powerfully effective leader or public servant who has not had to do that difficult personal work.

Knowing how to do something is a function of the conscious mind. The conscious mind, however, is not what holds the greatest influence over our behavior. Following through and putting knowledge into action, or praxis, is governed by our Emotion, which includes our sub-conscious beliefs. Just because you know how to do something doesn't mean that you do it. Managing reality fields is a valuable part of praxis.

Conscious thought, subconscious beliefs, and intuitive feelings must be in harmony in order for you to take effective action. You create this harmony by doing the necessary work to break through resistance and doubt and bring Thought, Emotion, and Truth into alignment. We live in a society that looks for someone to blame when things don't go according to plan. We are conditioned to look outside ourselves for the causes of problems. But as the sign on U.S. president

Harry S. Truman's desk read, "The buck stops here." Are we going to live in the Drama and Situation levels of engagement, or are we going to break through to Choice and Opportunity and be stewards of transformation? In the end, it is up to us to create and sustain the reality fields that will support who we are called to be and what we are called to do.

The most empowering choices in the alignment process require claiming personal responsibility—accepting that whatever is going wrong on the outside is most likely mirroring a conflict between your conscious thought and subconscious beliefs. This concept holds true at every level: personal, organizational, regional, and global. It is the Principle of Correspondence in action.

What still needs to shift for you, even though you're living consciously? Where is there still a gap between what you know and how you live? Be specific. Really examine these questions. We can rationalize anything, but if we want to close the gap and reach our greatest potential personally, organizationally, or globally, we must resist the urge to pass the buck. We must accept uncomfortable truths when they arise and address them. Doing so is living in integrity—bringing your Thought, Emotion, Truth, and actions into harmony. It is bringing the vertical and horizontal planes into congruence with one another.

Our personal challenges and successes mirror personal beliefs and behaviors, as well as societal beliefs and behaviors that we have adopted and made our own. Community challenges and successes mirror the community's mind-set and beliefs. National events and issues mirror the national mind-set and beliefs, and global events and issues mirror our global mind-set and beliefs. Regardless of the level, however, shifts can happen only as each of us, individually, uncovers what the larger issue is mirroring within us and chooses the necessary shifts in thoughts, beliefs, and behaviors. Shifts can happen only when we close the gaps.

Inquiry: Finding and Closing the Gaps in Your Life and Work
In deep process work, it can be very informative to consider the circumstances, situations, and relationships of our lives and work from

the perspective of "What if I created that? If, for a moment, I assume that I *did* create it, what new insight does this give me?" This perspective is not about creating blame or guilt. It is not about taking on more responsibility than is actually ours. It is about examining and accepting personal responsibility on a new level. Accepting responsibility for our part in creating our lives leads to empowerment.

By answering these questions, you begin to close the gaps between you and that situation. Addressing these gaps can allow you to tap into the situation from a very different perspective than you might ordinarily have. It can give you a much more complete understanding of the "what is," including its inherent potential, and lead to much more informed decisions and actions.

When problems or challenges arise, or when powerful emotions come to the surface, there is a potential trying to emerge. Albert Einstein invited us into the potential when he said that you cannot solve a problem from the same level of thinking at which it was created. If you insist on remaining in the same level of thinking, the problem will not get solved because you are choosing to live in the reality field of that problem or circumstance. The problem will continue to be sustained and supported by the reality field you broadcast. When you create a new reality field, you create the conditions for a new reality in which the problem does not exist. You create something wholly new.

So often I hear people talk about what they are trying to do. As soon as I hear the word *trying*, I know that there is a good chance that they will never actually do it. When you are *trying* to accomplish something, you are approaching it from the perspective of the problem or circumstance. Chances are you are caught in the Drama level of your current situation and, therefore, continue to feed energy to the emotions and thoughts that initially created and continue to sustain the circumstance. In this approach, there is at least some part of you that *does not actually believe* that what you are trying to accomplish is possible, but you are *trying* to make it so. Again, you are actually continuing to support the reality field of the problem and circumstance and encouraging things to stay the same. You are maintaining a gap. You may also be holding onto a sense of security that you feel will protect you or see you through the situation. Whether or not that security is real is irrelevant at the time. It is simply what you have known, or the spin you subconsciously need to put on the situation in order to convince yourself that you're on the right path.

On the other hand, when you create from potential, you reinforce the belief that you will accomplish your goal. You begin with a reality field that fully supports the potential. That reality field instantaneously calls forth new Emotion, Thought, and Truth because you are now vibrating to a new frequency. The circumstance does not yet exist in this reality. However, *it does exist in another reality*, and you must choose which reality you will engage. Which approach will you commit to? Will you close the gap?

When we embody a reality field, we become a part of the energy that makes up the field and, therefore, a part of what is created out of that field. We partner with the potential to cocreate an outcome. We step up to a new level of creative power, one that opens the door to a greatly expanded type of seeing and sensing: remembering the future. We close the gap that we previously perceived between us and the future, and we become one with the greatest potential of that future. We become the participant-observer, or the physical-realm partner, that is necessary for the potential to collapse from wave into particle—to take form in a three-dimensional reality. We are the bridge between energy and form. Our perceptions shift from being those of an observer to those of a cocreator giving birth to the future. We become totally present to what is emerging from the field of potential into a three-dimensional reality. Because we have created the reality field that, in part, makes that emergence possible, we join with potential to cocreate the outcome.

Inquiry: Gaps and Reality Fields
People's ability to hold a reality field can vary widely. You may find it easier to hold a reality field for an open parking space than for, say, increasing your income by $50,000 in the next year or for healing your body of a significant illness. Your capacity for stretching your

belief system, closing gaps, and sustaining reality fields is a significant determining factor in your success. Explore the following questions to learn more about your capacity for closing gaps and holding reality fields. Let yourself observe your responses without judgment. You are just gathering information. Then you will choose what to do with that information.

> In what areas of your life do you currently let potential guide your choices, actions, decisions? Do you find this challenging or easy? Or perhaps both challenging *and* easy?
> In what areas do you currently let your problems and circumstances guide your choice, actions, or decisions? How well does this serve you?
> In what areas of your life is it easy for you to hold a desired reality field? In what areas is it difficult?
> Based on your responses, what gaps are you observing?
> What do you now choose? How will you close the gaps?

An Ongoing Process
If we continue to stretch, grow, and evolve, new gaps will soon appear as we close old ones. Closing gaps is an ongoing process in transformational work, challenging us to recognize what we know, to live that knowledge, and then to step beyond that knowledge into the realm of quantum wisdom. When we discover new knowledge, we will find new gaps that we didn't even know existed. Closing the gaps challenges us to go beyond the classical-physics paradigm that says the only things there are to work with are what we have, and to recognize that there is more available to us beyond our current awareness.

Rarely finding gaps to close may be a sign that you are not challenging yourself to your full potential. Everyone has their edges, beyond which they are hesitant or even afraid to go. When you follow potential, the new edge and the gap between it and where you are will show up fairly quickly. The more you step into your role as cocreator of the future, the more you will actually create edges and gaps for yourself by challenging yourself to take the next leap, to explore the next frontier. And the more comfortable you become with seeing your own gaps as opportunities to reach your next level of potential, the more you will face the gaps with courage and confidence. In turn, you will more effectively help those you serve reach new levels of success and positive influence in the world. You become a master at cocreating the present and future. This is Transformational Presence.

Inquiry: Finding Your Edges

➤ Where is there an edge in your life? What is the gap that it represents?

➤ What edges have you not yet been willing to name? What will it take for you to name them and step across the corresponding gap? What is your level of commitment?

➤ Bring to mind those you serve. What are the edges some of them are coming up to? What do you recognize as possible edges that they may not yet have been willing to name? What are the gaps that those edges represent? What do you and/or they know about the other side of the gap? How can you help them step across the edge and close the gap?

CHAPTER TWENTY-TWO

A World Transformed

It's not time for revolutions. Now is not the moment to fight
against the old. We need to step away from that which doesn't
work and begin to create that which works—to enter into
evolution.

—TOKE MØLLER, *cofounder and CEO, InterChange ApS*

Toke Møller's words above sum up both this time in history and the
essence of Transformational Presence work. The time for fighting
against the old has past. Now is the time for partnering with potential
as an active participant in our forward evolution. We have the opportunity to be bridges of understanding between ideas and principles;
yet more than that, we can be bridges of understanding between our
future and our present and between our present and our past. We
have the opportunity to listen to the potentials waiting to unfold for
a greater good. Some of those potentials are already emerging, and
our job is simply to partner with them and move forward. Others
are still deeply hidden under the challenges, conflicts, and conditions
we and those we serve find ourselves in. Transformational Presence
provides a bridge that allows the greatest potential of our future to
become reality now.

We began this journey with the Four Levels of Engagement and
making Choice and Opportunity our habitual approach to life. I
spoke of standing in Choice and Opportunity while observing the
dramas and situations all around us and within us, so that we can
discover what is really wanting to happen, what hidden potential is

222 CREATE A WORLD THAT WORKS

trying to get our attention. From there, we explored living on many levels of awareness at once, habitually engaging as many facets of the intuitive mind as we possibly can. Living and working from this expanded awareness allows us to feel and understand the what is of those we serve without getting caught up in it.

Transformational Presence means meeting those we serve with humility, compassion, and an open heart, all the while holding the space for a new reality that is waiting to emerge. We can listen to their words to learn their language—the words that will make sense to them—and then, speaking their language, invite them into a relationship with the what is that will truly serve them and create a new reality. If they are not in crisis, we can help them tap into the next great potential waiting to unfold and turn that potential into reality. If they are in crisis, we can help them address their immediate needs and then call them to their greatest inner power. And we can learn from them, for deep inside, they hold a greater wisdom about their own circumstances and conditions than we might imagine.

Creating a world that works requires Transformational Presence. It requires alignment with the heights and depths of the vertical plane and actively engaging that alignment to inform and guide actions and new creation in the horizontal plane. It demands a willingness to step into once-and-for-all commitments. It demands a commitment to evolving potential at both the personal and cultural levels. It invites commitment to the action and cocreation that the potential asks for. Making a difference through Transformational Presence means calling those you serve to find their greatest gifts, skills, and passions and holding space for their magnificence to shine.

Creating a world that works requires living in an ongoing dialogue with emerging potential and Consciousness in order to serve the greatest good of all. It requires partnership and cocreation. It requires recognizing clearly your part in our ongoing evolutionary process—what is yours to do and, equally important, what is *not* yours to do—and helping those you serve do the same. When you insist on doing what is not yours to do, you cheat others out of the opportunity to share their gifts and make their offerings. Trust that there is someone for every job, be clear about what job is yours to do, and call colleagues and those you serve to their greatness by helping them step into the jobs that are truly theirs to do.

Creating a world that works requires holding those we serve big— holding them in their greatness, not in their challenges, conflicts, crisis, or stuckness. Hold them in their greatest potential, even when they are not yet able to do so. That's a huge part of why we are there—to hold the vision and partner with the potential even when they can't. That is service. That is leadership.

In my training programs for coaches and leaders, the most frequently asked question, especially early on in the program, is, how can you possibly use these approaches in the mainstream world? Here is where Transformational Presence is critical. We cannot transform anyone. But we can create an optimal space for those who are ready to transform. Our job is not to convince anyone of anything. Our job is to notice where the next opening for transformational service is emerging and be present for that service. The early signs of emerging potential may be well-disguised, but as you pay attention to what is happening on many levels of awareness, you may be surprised to find that the mainstream world is more ready for these ideas and approaches than you had thought.

Your job is to live the principles of Transformational Presence. If you stand confidently in your Transformational Presence, people will find you when they are ready. And when they see that there is no gap between what you say and how you live, when they can see that you totally believe in what you are sharing with them, and when they can see that your life works, they will come with you. Every person you serve is a person with a heart and a soul. And deep inside, everyone has a yearning to be seen, heard, and recognized for who they are and what they have to offer. When you are authentic and confident in who you are and believe in what you are doing, and your focus is on service and seeing those you serve in their wisdom and magnificence, they will come with you. Allow time for trust to build. Establish relationships, and stand in that balance of love and power that was spoken about in the first chapter. Take these tools and concepts and adapt them in whatever ways you need for the moment. Put them into a language and approach that those you serve will be able to hear and understand, and invite them into discovery. By doing so, you will open doors to new possibilities and new realities that may never have been imagined.

Finally, Transformational Presence is an art. Creating a world that works is an art. Nothing in this book is a hard and fast formula or model. Everything here is a vehicle or a tool to get you and those you serve to a new place of awareness and discovery. Therefore, let this book become a foundation of knowledge and understanding from which you lead and serve. Create your own tools or variations on the ones presented here. In my own coaching practice, I have found that if I keep just three big concepts in mind—the Four Levels of Engagement, the Vertical and Horizontal Planes of Awareness, and the Potential-Based Approach—I have what I need to help those I serve achieve great things. Everything we have explored is held within those three big concepts. Beyond that, it is a matter of listening deeply and letting the potential show us the way. As those I serve learn to do the same thing, our work together becomes an amazing unfolding of discovery, cocreation, breakthroughs, and great accomplishment.

It is my hope that, through this book, you have taken significant steps into your own Transformational Presence. Keep using the book over and over again until these principles and concepts are the backbone of your life, leadership, and service. Stand tall in your unique and powerful Transformational Presence, give to the world that which is truly yours to give, and support others to do the same. Together, we really can create a world that works.

BIBLIOGRAPHY

Books

Abram, David. *The Spell of the Sensuous.* New York: Vintage Books, 1997.

Braden, Gregg. *Awakening to Zero Point.* N.p.: Sacred Spaces/ Ancient Wisdom, 1997.

———. *The God Code.* Carlsbad, CA: Hay House, 2004.

———. *The Isaiah Effect.* New York: Three Rivers Press, 2000.

———. *The Divine Matrix.* Carlsbad, CA: Hay House, 2007.

Capra, Fritjof. *The Tao of Physics.* Boston: Shambhala Publications, 1975.

Childre, Doc, with Howard Martin and Donna Beech. *The Heart-Math Solution.* New York: HarperCollins Publishers, 1999.

Chittister, Joan. *Scarred by Struggle, Transformed by Hope.* Grand Rapids, MI: William B. Eerdmans Publishing, 2003.

Dyer, Wayne. *Wisdom of the Ages.* New York: HarperCollins Publishers, 1998.

Emoto, Masaru. *The Hidden Messages in Water.* Hillsboro, OR: Beyond Words Publishing, 2004.

———. *The True Power of Water: Healing and Discovering Ourselves.* Hillsboro, OR: Beyond Words Publishing, 2005.

Gibran, Kahlil. *The Prophet.* Available online on the website *Leb.net* (http://leb.net/~mira/works/prophet/prophet.html).

Gladwell, Malcolm. *The Tipping Point.* New York: Little, Brown, and Company, 2002.

Goodall, Jane. *Reason for Hope.* New York: Warner Books, 2000.

Hahn, Thich Nhat. *The Art of Power.* New York: HarperOne, 2007.

Jaworski, Joseph. *Synchronicity: The Inner Path of Leadership.* San Francisco: Berrett-Koehler Publishers, 1996.

Kimura, Yasuhiko Genko. *Think Kosmically, Act Globally.* Waynes-
boro, VA: University of Science and Philosophy, 2000.

Kinkade, Amelia. *The Language of Miracles.* Novato, CA: New
World Library, 2006.

Laszlo, Ervin. *Science and the Akashic Field.* Rochester, VT: Inner
Traditions, 2004.

Leonard, George. *Mastery: The Keys to Success and Long-Term Fulfill-
lment.* New York: Plume, 1992.

———. *The Way of Aikido: Life Lessons from an American Sensei.* New
York: Plume, 2000.

Levine, Stephen. *A Gradual Awakening.* New York: Anchor Books,
1979.

———. *Healing into Life and Death.* New York: Anchor Books,
1989.

McTaggart, Lynne. *The Field: The Quest for the Secret Force of the
Universe.* New York: HarperCollins, 2002.

Morehouse, David. *The Remote Viewing Training Course.* Boulder,
CO: Sounds True, 2004.

Plotkin, Bill. *Soulcraft: Crossing into the Mysteries of Nature and Psyche.* Novato, CA: New World Library, 2003.

Radin, Dean I. *The Conscious Universe: The Scientific Truth of Psychic
Phenomena.* New York: Harper One, 2009.

———. *Entangled Minds: Extrasensory Experiences in a Quantum
Reality.* New York: Paraview Pocket Books, 2006.

Ram Dass. *Still Here: Embracing Aging, Changing, and Dying.* New
York: Riverhead Books, 2001.

Rodegast, Pat, and Judith Stanton. *Emmanuel's Book: A Manual
for Living Comfortably in the Cosmos.* New York: Bantam Books,
1987.

———. *Emmanuel's Book II: The Choice for Love.* New York: Bantam
Books, 1997.

———. *Emmanuel's Book III: What Is an Angel Doing Here?* New
York: Bantam Books, 1994.

Roosevelt, Eleanor, and David Emblidge, editor. *My Day: The Best
of Eleanor Roosevelt's Acclaimed Newspaper Columns, 1936–1962.*
Cambridge, MA: Da Capo Press, 2001.

Schlitz, Marilyn Mandala. *Living Deeply: The Art & Science of Transformation in Everyday Life.* Oakland: New Harbinger Publications, Inc., 2007.

Schnable, Jim. *Remote Viewers: The Secret History of America's Psychic Spies.* New York: Bantam Doubleday Dell, 1997.

Seale, Alan. *Intuitive Living.* San Francisco: Weiser Books, 2001

———. *The Manifestation Wheel.* San Francisco: Weiser Books, 2007.

———. *Soul Mission, Life Vision.* Boston: Red Wheel, 2003.

Senge, Peter, et al. *Presence: Human Purpose and the Field of Potential.* Cambridge, MA: The Society for Organizational Learning, 2004.

Stevens, Jose, and Lena Stevens. *The Power Path: The Shaman's Way to Success in Business and Life.* Novato, CA: New World Library, 2002.

Three Initiates. *The Kybalion: Hermetic Philosophy.* N.p.: Yogi Publication Society, 1940.

Twist, Lynne. *The Soul of Money.* New York: W.W. Norton & Company, 2003.

Washington, James. *A Testament of Hope: The Essential Writings and Speeches of Martin Luther King, Jr.* New York: HarperCollins, 1991.

Waters, Frank. *The Book of the Hopi.* Ballantine Books, 1963.

Zander, Rosamund Stone, and Benjamin Zander. *The Art of Possibility.* New York: Penguin Books, 2002.

Articles

Bodine, Tobias. "The Invisible School: The Art of Cultural Mentoring." *Shift,* no. 8 (September–November 2005): 24.

Carroll, Laura. "The World Is Teaching Me." *Shift,* no. 8 (September–November 2005): 23.

Diebold, Elizabeth. "Spiritual But Not Religious: Moving Beyond Postmodern Spirituality." *What Is Enlightenment?* (December 2005–February 2006): 61.

Marshall, Stephanie Page. "A Decidedly Different Mind," *Shift,* no. 8 (September–November 2005): 12.

Said, Abdul Aziz. "Growing Global Citizens." *Shift*, no. 8 (September–November 2005): 20.

Stahma, Barbara. "Biology is Belief: A Conversation with Bruce Lipton." *Science of Mind* 78, no. 10 (October 2005): 78.

Online Sources

Captured Light Distribution and the Institute for Noetic Sciences. *What the Bleep Do We Know? Study Guide*. Study guide for the 2004 film of the same name. Available on the website *What the Bleep Do We Know?*, *www.whatthebleep.com*.

IONS: Institute of Noetic Sciences, website for the organization of the same name. *www.noetic.org*.

Other

Heuerman, Tom. "Personal Leadership: The Call to Nobility," a speech to educators. October 2003.

IONS: Institute of Noetic Sciences *Shift in Action* member audio series. Available by subscription at the website *Shift in Action*, *www.shiftinaction.com*.

Rein, Glen, and Rollin McCraty, *Modulation of DNA by Coherent Heart Frequencies*. Proceedings of the Third Annual Conference of the International Society for the Study of Subtle Energies and Energy Medicine, Monterey, CA, June 1993.

The Center for Transformational Presence
Alan Seale, Founder and Director

The Center for Transformational Presence is a discovery, learning, development, and transformation environment for individuals and organizations who are committed to making a significant difference in their world. Our clients and program participants are social and spiritual visionaries, leaders, and coaches who are committed to doing their part to create a world that works. They include social entrepreneurs, executives, managers, government leaders, educators, spiritual teachers, coaches, healers, and anyone who is ready to hold themselves and/or their organizations accountable for the future.

The Center offers leadership coaching as well as courses and training programs in Transformational Presence Coaching, Transformational Leadership, Soul Mission, Manifestation, and Personal Presence. For more information, visit *www.transformationalpresence.org.*

About the Author

MAUREEN EDWARDS

Alan Seale is a leadership and transformation coach, inspirational speaker, and the founder and director of the Center for Transformational Presence. He serves on the faculties of the International Coach Academy and CoachWalk Academy in Sweden and is a visiting lecturer at the Graduate Institute in Connecticut. Alan maintains a full workshop schedule throughout North America and Europe and serves coaching clients from five continents who are committed to making a significant difference in their world. For more about Alan, see *www.transformationalpresence.org.*

ALSO BY ALAN SEALE:

Intuitive Living: A Sacred Path

Soul Mission, Life Vision: Recognize Your True Gifts and Make Your Mark in the World

The Manifestation Wheel: A Practical Process for Creating Miracles

The Power of Your Presence